BE CONFIDENT!

Réamonn Ó Donnchadha

Newleaf

Newleaf

an imprint of
Gill & Macmillan Ltd
Hume Avenue
Park West
Dublin 12
with associated companies throughout the world
www.gillmacmillan.ie

© Réamonn Ó Donnchadha 2002
0 7171 3365 6
Print origination by Carole Lynch, Dublin
Printed by ColourBooks Ltd, Dublin

This book is typeset in 11/14pt Bembo

The paper used in this book is made from the wood pulp of managed forests.
For every tree felled, at least one tree is planted, thereby renewing natural resources.

A catalogue record is available for this book from the British Library.

1 3 5 4 2

CONTENTS

INTRODUCTION

·◞

One of the most salient features of our world today is the developing importance of therapists, counsellors, personal assistants, life trainers and all manner of 'helpers'. The subliminal message is that people are unable to 'look after' themselves, that we all need someone to help us and that adults never leave the dependence of childhood behind. Side by side with this is the notion, mostly in the male world but increasingly in the psyche of the woman, that asking for help is a sign of weakness, that self-reliance and independence are the badges of personal happiness and that admitting mistakes is 'a bad thing'. Additionally, the idea that the family is responsible for passing on social, personal and emotional skills is somehow being neglected. The combination of less time being spent together by parents and children, the perception that life is more complicated for today's children than it was for us when we were children, and the subsequent growth in helping professions have all combined to take away the responsibility for transmitting life skills from parents and ultimately created doubts about our ability to cope in our own world.

Each of the above is in its own way contributing to a situation where we as individuals are losing sight of the innate, inherited capability we all have within us, to survive. The helper syndrome is gradually producing a learned helplessness in society which will lead to an unwillingness and perhaps an inability to survive and to cope with life.

On the other hand, in this world of greed and unfettered individualism, the superperson syndrome, characterised by people who don't cry, don't need help and never show weakness, is gradually isolating us from our inner resources, from the support of extended family, and from the established structures of society. As a result, a genuine need has emerged for counselling and therapy.

This book is about enabling individuals to discover and use their own inherited and unused strength. It is about the idea that we possess the ability to live our lives effectively and in a way that makes us feel we have a say in what happens to us. The book explores the idea, put forward by Carl Jung, that each person is not just a separate individual, but inherits an accumulated pool of wisdom from ancestors, parents, grandparents and extended family. How effectively we tap into this genetic super-highway is to some extent controlled by the way in which we have been treated as children, at home and in school. As adults the responsibility for accessing this inner well of survival skills is in our own hands.

This book brings readers on a journey through their own psyche, a journey of discovery of their own hidden resources, and invites them to become aware of who they are and what they are capable of.

The book is also an invitation to readers to look for help, to accept it and yet to know that it is within themselves that the greatest help is to be found.

1

THE SELF

THE PERSONA

As we grow through childhood we learn that some behaviours are acceptable; these behaviours help us achieve what we want, so that we can survive in a way that satisfies our view of ourselves in our world. In other words certain behaviours gain us approval from the significant people in our world, and we are encouraged to repeat them in the expectation of receiving more approval. As a rule we tend to repeat such behaviours and where these are acceptable and rewarded they become the outer cover or persona that we present to society as we go through life. The word persona means 'mask' and refers to a mask worn by actors. It is used to convey the idea of hiding our real identity and putting forward a side of ourselves that we have found to be acceptable, and that we expect to be acceptable to those who matter in our lives.

We know that this accumulation of behaviours will gain approval from society and we are therefore at ease with presenting it to the outer world. Our persona is a functional part of the personality, developed to enable us to adapt to society. It is the role that we characteristically play when relating to others. This accumulation of acceptable layers of behaviour, attitudes and ideas is in effect the wrapper on the real person, and it functions as the person's public relations package. It makes our relationships easier at work, at home, and in our world generally because it is our accommodation to what society demands of us in order that we can be accepted as being a doctor, a teacher, a garda, a nurse etc. in society.

While the persona or mask is essentially a good thing and is developed for survival reasons, it is not the real person nor is it the entire personality. If we develop a persona which is too far removed from the real person, we will become insecure and unhappy because the real person behind the persona does not have the personality to sustain the demands being made by keeping up such an imposed public face.

Another difficulty can arise where we identify totally with our persona. This happens where individuals are so identified with the work they do, so attached to the public perception of their job, that there is no separation of the persona from the actual self. What happens in this case is that all other parts of the personality are denied and the individual finds it difficult to relate to people at a feeling, emotional or human level. The person who is all persona will be too concerned with what people think and will have no real separate identity.

Initially the persona grows out of a need to adapt to the expectations and demands of parents, teachers and society in general in the course of growing up. The underlying need to survive and the innate skill of doing what is necessary to survive, means that children quickly learn that certain behaviours are desirable. The desirable and approved behaviours and ideas will gradually be incorporated into the personality as children internalise them and these become a part of their psychological make-up. In short the persona is a collective or universal facet of our make-up, a part of each of us that might easily belong to someone else. The importance of the persona is seen where a person fails to develop a persona. Such a person will be gauche, unaware of social niceties, will find it difficult to fit in and will offend others easily.

THE SHADOW

At the same time as the process of developing a persona is happening there is a simultaneous hiding, covering, repressing and generally keeping secret of those aspects of behaviour, ideas, responses and attitudes that are perceived as undesirable, unrewarding and not likely to gain approval from the significant others in our lives.

These hidden negative dispositions come to form the shadow, which develops in a similar fashion to the persona. However, the shadow includes the denial of some of our natural characteristics while the persona includes the embracing of some traits that come easily. The shadow is the counterbalance to the persona. It grows and develops in the same psyche as the persona. It is therefore very closely connected both in content and effect with the persona. The most significant aspect of the shadow is that it possesses traits, ideas and contents which are opposite to those manifested in the persona. Interestingly, both shadow and persona are different for all people even for children who grow up in the same family.

When we hear somebody make the excuse 'I don't know what came over me' or 'I was not myself', we are seeing the shadow in action. The shadow is the inferior side of our personality, the negative aspect of our being, the highly individual and instinctual side that society has conditioned us to keep out of sight. The shadow is in a part of us, our unconscious, which is hidden from us, and it is here that we consign all those aspects of behaviour, feeling and emotion that we consider to be unacceptable. In the same way as young children learn what is acceptable and what behaviours will gain approval, the behaviours that they find to be unacceptable to others are hidden in a part of the psyche where they won't have to come face to face with them. This is a healthy act of survival which individuals need in order to gain acceptance in the family and in society. However, although the shadow is out of sight, and for the most part, out of mind, it is very much a living, growing, influential part of the inner workings of the psyche. The contents of the shadow, which are the rejected aspects of the individual, carry a sense of personal identity and continue to be active, rather like a volcano. In times of crisis, vulnerability, or when the psyche is not well defended as in sleep, the shadow will manifest itself.

As more and more layers are added to the shadow, we become less and less acquainted with its contents and are therefore more and more ashamed and embarrassed when faced with it. Because the contents of our shadow are in the main unconscious and we therefore are unaware that they are there, it is possible to hide the shadow and to avoid facing it. As we grow, we develop successful ways of doing this, which means that there is a considerable part of our psyche that we are unaware of.

Knowing who we are should be one of the easiest tasks in life. Perhaps it may be that we should know without having to find out. However, there are so many influences that go to make up the individual, and so many unconscious defences we have developed to avoid having to come face to face with our own real self, that unless we make a conscious effort to get behind the public self we may never know the real person. As we grow and go through life we encounter many experiences, people and events which we find so hurtful and damaging that we are unable to face them. So we develop strategies to help us to cope, or more correctly to avoid having to face them. As a result our real self becomes buried underneath the false self of our defences.

We develop many strategies for protecting ourselves from the pain and discomfort of unpleasant experiences. Our basic and most important need is to survive, and to do this we often have to avoid social or emotional damage, which happens if we do not live up to our own view of what is needed to maintain our personal emotional standing in relation to our environment. This refers to how we see ourselves in our family, in our workplace or among our friends. The need to survive is much more than physical survival. It includes being able to live with ourselves emotionally, being able to maintain our status in the workplace, and being comfortable in the company of friends. We need to be able to do all these in a way that is acceptable to our own sense of who we are and who we ideally would like to be.

An important aspect of the developing of defences is that it relates to the underlying feeling of inadequacy and inferiority in terms of dealing with the particular perceived threat. It is more to do with the sense of our own emotional and experiential competence than it has to do with the level of difficulty or complexity of a particular event, environment or person which is perceived by us as being the reason for the fear.

Defence mechanisms are sometimes damaging in that they do not help us to adapt, they do not allow us to face our negative side and they prevent us from real personal growth. They are more often than not an unconscious reaction, meaning that we are not deliberately taking evasive action to avoid facing the psychic danger.

RUNNING AWAY

The most effective way we have of avoiding painful experiences is by running away or simply avoiding the situation that we think is likely to cause us anxiety. We develop strategies for running away from situations where we are experiencing discomfort, or where we anticipate either psychological or physical discomfort, on the basis of previous experience. We find reasons for not going to the party, reasons for not meeting the person or reasons for not going to work. These reasons may be very good reasons but are often not the real reason.

A very simple example of this is when we see a person approaching and we either look the other way or cross the street to avoid him or her. We decide, sometimes consciously, and sometimes unconsciously, that it is 'safer' for us to avoid the person, based on what we know of him or her, and what effect we expect this to have on us, as a result of our previous experience of meeting this person. Such avoidance behaviour is, to us, necessary at that time, and is at that time positive, or good, for us. Where the behaviour can become damaging is if it continues and becomes completely unconscious. It has then been assimilated into our psyche and it becomes damaging to our personal development.

REPRESSION

Repression is a form of running away that is more psychological than physical. Here the person deliberately or otherwise pushes the anxiety-inducing thoughts or experiences into the unconscious. Though this will get rid of the anxiety in the short term and may be necessary for the immediate survival of the person, the anxiety and personal unease are really only sent to another part of the psyche. It is consigned to the personal unconscious of the individual and has not been dealt with. It therefore remains as an influencing factor in the life of the person. It is rather like the delete function on the computer. The unwanted, uncomfortable issues are not visible but they are there. One of the most damaging aspects of repression is that the issues, attitudes and ideas that are pushed into the 'recycle bin' of the unconscious will not be exposed to the reality testing of the outside world and will there-fore never be challenged or changed. Because these shadow issues are never exposed to the challenge of reality, they never get the chance to grow and will remain at the infantile level of develop-ment, until they are forcibly taken out and addressed. This means that when they do appear in times of stress, vulnerability or unguarded unconscious moments, they appear in our behaviour as primeval, instinctual and undeveloped incidents of behaviour that are damaging and dangerous.

PROJECTION

Another way we have of avoiding painful situations or our own feelings of inadequacy is by projection. This is a process whereby we are unwilling to see our own faults and tend to attribute them to others. It is easier for us to find fault in others than in ourselves. Children use projection very effectively to help them avoid taking responsibility for their own shortcomings. We often hear a child say, 'He made me do it'! The projection of our own negative feel-ings, behaviours and attitudes on to others has many advantages for us, not least of which is that it allows us to see ourselves as we would like to see ourselves. However, as in other defences, while it may have a short-term beneficial effect, its real consequence is to take away the need for us to change our behaviour. A husband or wife will almost certainly find it distasteful or unacceptable to acknowledge anger at some aspect of personal behaviour, and will more easily attribute the anger to the other partner. The person who laments that 'everybody in this office is so devious and greedy,' may well be drawing attention to his or her own deviousness and greed.

DAYDREAMING

Daydreaming is a common survival mechanism in children and adults. It allows them to lapse into what is a very selfish fantasy where they can escape the unpleasant feelings associated with bad experiences. Again it is evident that daydreaming has a short-term beneficial function in that it provides us with an escape from the immediately perceived threat, but if resorted to continuously would mean that we would never engage with the reality of the world.

INTELLECTUALISATION

Intellectualisation is a common defence against having to face up to unpleasant feelings. This involves excessive abstract thinking and grandiose talking about the subject as a way of not having to experience anxiety-laden people or events. This has the 'advantage' of making us feel that we are actually doing something about the problem while in fact we are avoiding any emotional or experiential contact with the danger.

Intellectualisation may surface in any situation but it is more often seen where the person is attempting to confront the shadow. Talk can easily become a defence against dealing with issues, or an escape from listening, and because it, loosely, comes under the heading of doing something it is easily used as a substitute for dealing with issues.

DISPLACEMENT

Displacement occurs where there is a perceived threat from an event, person or situation that seems bigger and more powerful than ourselves. The feeling of danger and fear is dealt with by displacing or redirecting it on to another usually less threatening object. This has the effect of making us feel that the threat is more manageable. While such behaviour has the effect of giving immediate relief from the stressful situation, if we become habituated to its use we continue to avoid the issue that is causing us distress, we continue to pretend that it is really something else that is causing us the problem, and we never take the risk of addressing the real issue.

DENIAL

Denial occurs when we fail to acknowledge, or apparently fail to notice, some negative aspect of the real world even though this is evident to all around us. The underlying and unconscious basis for denial is that the perceived threat to our emotional world is too painful to face, and it is only by pretending that it 'never happened' that we can feel safe. Continued denial leads to living in an unreal world where nothing bad ever happens, and where the person is never exposed to the reality testing of real experience and so does not learn to survive.

IDEALISATION

Idealisation most often occurs between people who are closely linked such as parents and children, and it involves us attributing unrealistic and exaggeratedly positive qualities to another person. It prevents us from ever seeing the reality of the person and also from having a realistic concept of ourselves. This is a form of defence that allows us to avoid our own flaws and inferior side, because all our energies, good and bad, are invested in the other person. All our success and failure are determined by the success or failure of the person we idealise. Not only is the identity of the idealised person subsumed, but the identity of the idealising person is also fused with the other.

REGRESSION

Regression is a defence mechanism whereby we retreat to the behaviour and reactions and language that we associate with a time when we were younger and which worked as a protective and secure device.

ADDICTION

One of the most common ways of hiding the shadow is through addiction. We become addicted to many different types of behaviour. The more visible addictions such as addictions to alcohol or drugs are perhaps the most widely acknowledged but there are many other ways in which we become addicted to avoid acknowledging the issues in our shadow side.

Many people become addicted to their work as a means of escaping from the feeling side of life. Such individuals will probably have an overdeveloped persona, will identify too closely with their profession and be over-eager to please other people in the workplace. Work addiction has the attraction of being an addiction to an activity that is intrinsically good, and this is in fact its main difficulty, because it is easy to justify being addicted to something that is necessary for survival.

Arising out of the greed and competitiveness of our society, there is a growing inability to 'be' and a compulsion to 'do'. This manifests itself in the way in which as adults we are continually doing something, always engaged in some activity and always having some form of distraction in our lives such as listening to the radio, watching television or reading the paper. The pressure to do well at school and to achieve in life has created a spurious need among parents to drive their children and to hothouse them in terms of education and general personal achievement. This need is being fuelled by a fear among parents that their child will miss out or be left behind and somehow not 'make it', and the result is that children are forced to spend every waking moment involved in activities that will give them an edge. They never have any time on their own. They are always supervised, chaperoned, and kept active. They are never allowed to be bored. This 'addiction to distraction' is both damaging and contagious in that children never learn to value their own company and they develop a life-long discomfort with the idea of being on their own.

A close relative of addiction to distraction is addiction to perfection which manifests itself in the way in which we are uncomfortable with mistakes and find it difficult to accept things or people that do not appear perfect. This has its roots in our desire to avoid imperfections in our own inner selves and our attempts to compensate for this by having our environment perfect.

THE IMPORTANCE OF KNOWING OUR SHADOW

The shadow is the weakest aspect of our make-up because it represents something about ourselves that we are either unwilling or unable to acknowledge, and that therefore remains in our unconscious. Though we are unaware of what issues we have hidden in our shadow, it is an active, important part of our psychological make-up, which as long as it is unacknowledged remains unused, undeveloped and therefore damaging to our whole person.

And yet, our shadow is also our strongest point in that, when we acknowledge what we have hidden, become conscious of these negative aspects of our make-up, and accept them as part of who we are, then we can confront them and deal with them. It is at this point, when we begin to deal with our own shadow, that we begin to change and to grow. Knowing who we really are involves getting past the false self, the outer shell or shield of attitudes, prejudices and behaviours that 'protect' the real self.

It is important to keep in mind that it has taken until now for each of us to become who we are. It has taken until now for the shadow, persona and real self to achieve their present level of development and influence in our individual lives. It is understandable that when we suddenly become aware of these negative aspects of our make-up, we want immediate change. Just as the development of the persona and the shadow have taken time, unravelling them will also take time.

THE WAYS OF KNOWING OUR SHADOW

➤ Our reaction to issues or behaviours of other people will tell us what our shadow issues are. The important point here is that the reaction belongs to us. We own it, and it is always difficult for us to separate the reaction from the cause of the reaction.

The behaviour or issue that causes us to react in a certain way may belong to others but our reaction to it tells us that it is we who have a difficulty with this. The strength of our reaction, the duration of its existence, and the difficulty we experience in leaving the reaction aside, all tell us about the strength and level of undevelopment of our shadow.

➤ The things that bother us most in other people are often the things that we are most uncomfortable with in our own personality. It is the difficulty we have in accepting traits, values and attitudes in our own make-up that makes us so unaccepting of them in others.

➤ The things we least like to think about are also an indication of those areas in ourselves that we are uncomfortable with, and that therefore we do not want to think about. We see this in operation if we take note of how, when we are sitting 'idly' on our own, and suddenly for no immediately conscious reason we get up and move to do something else. It is usually the uncomfortable thought that has caused us to move.

➤ Becoming aware of and admitting our strengths provides the necessary balance to acknowledging the shadow. It is important to allow time to identify the things you are good at and to acknowledge that you can do these things. Share your achievements with others, particularly those close to you. The ability to be who you are involves being able to acknowledge your positive aspects, and not being embarrassed by others drawing attention to your talents. It is often seen as negative or boastful to take pride in our achievements and where this becomes internalised and assimilated it can manifest itself as a negative aspect in our behaviour. This negative internal picture of ourselves can have its origins in childhood and if through parenting, teaching and other forms of 'positive' conditioning, we internalise and assimilate a negative view of our positive aspects we may, as adults, find it hard to break out of the negative shell of self-criticism and low self-worth.

➤ Hand in hand with this positive affirmation is the value of acknowledging our weaknesses. Knowing our weaknesses, not attributing these flaws to others, and accepting ownership is an essential part of the process of learning who we are, and of being happy with that. In learning and accepting our weaknesses and our strengths it is good to accept that our weaknesses are not the totality of ourselves. They are only a part of our overall make-up and it is by accepting them and taking them on as a real part of ourselves that we can take away their power.

➤ Separate what we can do from who we are. What we do is only one aspect of our make-up and it is easy to become identified with our role, our job or our family. While all of these help to make up the overall psychological package of the person, it is important to separate our personal self from the persona of our work as a business person, a doctor, a cleaner, a nurse, a painter, a farmer etc. Being able to separate our behaviour from who we are is especially important in regard to negative behaviour. Owning our behaviour is essential but acknowledging that it is only one aspect of who we are is equally important.

PAT'S STORY

Pat is in his fifties, married with children. He grew up in rural Ireland where sexuality was never spoken about, and any mention of it was not only discouraged but punished. Violence in the home was commonplace and there was no real emotional connection between father and son. Pat's life was one of loneliness, guilt and fear about his sexuality and he was never able to communicate this to others. As a young man growing up any experience of a sexual nature was hidden and if discovered, punished. His adult life was dominated by fear and was marked by periods of absenteeism, abandonment, drinking and depression.

When his own children were born, his fears became personified in them and as they grew up they took on some of the traits and fears of the father. In relationships he was aloof, distant and closed and was unable to communicate. His fear of communication was based on his deeply felt guilt and a dread that people would find out what he had done, that he would be shamed, and that he would be to blame if his children turned out like him. His family was ensnared in his web of unhappiness and anger and began to fulfil the prophetic fear that he had.

Gradually he became more and more worried that his children were going to become what he had been and he sought help. It was more for his children that he sought help than for himself. This revealed certain aspects: how Pat was unwilling to put himself first, his difficulty in asking for help, his lack of feelings of self worth, and the way in which his adult problems manifested themselves through his children. Pat had a deep sense of shame and embarrassment about his life and in particular about his sexuality, and this was exacerbated by the guilt he had as a result of feeling that he had made his children the same as he was.

The underlying unhappiness and guilt that Pat had endured for most of his adult life had manifested itself as lack of interest, isolation from his family, dependency on drink, and depression.

The therapy sessions were marked initially by long silences, feelings of discomfort for Pat, resistance and fear of being 'found out'. Much of the difficulty revolved around embarrassment, shame and unwillingness to expose what lay beneath the surface. It was important for Pat to allow the silence to continue as long as he liked, to be comfortable with it, and to accept it as a form of communication.

Working with Pat, the key element was the development of trust and the gradual realisation that the trust which had been damaged as a child and which he thought was lost forever, could in fact be built up in the safety of the therapy room. Many of the sessions we had together were spent talking about farming, animals, nature and aspects of life which, it appeared, had nothing to do with why we were there. But this was for Pat a necessary testing of my acceptance of him as he was, and it was through this that he moved towards acceptance of himself as he was.

Reaching inside to his negative side and being able to talk about parts of his life that up to now were simply too painful to even think about, was the turning point. It was helped by knowing that his behaviour was not him, but a part of him. It was also helped by knowing that if he could test it on me and if I could accept it without judgement, then it was possible that it wasn't so bad after all. The relief and feeling of power he felt was sufficient motivation to continue.

One of the most noticeable differences was in the way he walked. It was as if a weight had been lifted from him. His step became lighter, his walk became more purposeful and he seemed to become a different person.

His depression had lifted.

_____

2

INHERITED
WISDOM

I n the work of Carl Jung we learn of the concept of the collective unconscious, a term he uses to explain how we all have
access to a pool of genetically inherited wisdom. The content
of the collective unconscious is a growing expanding well of
knowledge which is contributed to by each generation and each
member of the generation as it passes through. Each of us not only
contributes to this but also has access to it during our own lives.

In approaching the real self of the person and in accessing the
inner worth of the individual there are a number of aspects of the
overall person which we should consider. The outer shell of the
persona has its uses and acts as a protection against isolation and
alienation. Having a healthy persona enables us to be accepted by
society and to belong to the community. Inability to develop a persona leaves a person outside the boundary of society, excluded. The
real person, however, is not the persona but is behind the outer
layer of socially acceptable behaviours that we adopt in order to
fit in to society. To find the real, true, personal self we need to peel
back the persona and recognise the unfamiliar.

It is not only the persona that hides the real self from the world
and from the person. As we have seen, the shadow or negative side
of the person is also an aspect of the overall person that is not
usually visible to the outer world. If we are to come to know and
accept the real self it is necessary to acknowledge, accept and
integrate the shadow side.

In addition to the shadow and the persona of the person there is a hidden aspect to the overall personality which is more difficult to tap into. There is a part of the unconscious psyche which contains aspects of behaviour, habits, ideas and wisdom that come to us through the collective unconscious. The collective unconscious is that part of our make-up which has been handed down to us through the accumulated learning and experiences of our families, our extended family and our community. The way in which previous generations experienced the world, the way they reacted to their environment, the way they succeeded in shaping their world, and the lessons and wisdom acquired through this are all internalised and passed on through generations. This learning and wisdom is part of the genetic package that is filtered, shaped and passed on. It can lie dormant in the unconscious until particular experiences, be they emotional or physical, cause them to be activated. These unconscious contents can also be tapped into by using what is termed intuition.

Intuition is often defined as unconscious learning, knowing something though not being conscious of having learned it. It can best be described as instinctive knowing without the constraints of logic. It is often our very first reaction to a situation, our immediate response without conscious thinking, our own genuine and untainted view of the situation. It is often quite difficult to heed our intuition as it seems to be irrational, impractical and unworkable. The enemy of intuition is our logical, thinking, judging side and the more we apply logic to what intuition is telling us the more difficult it is to act on our intuition. The value of our intuition is that it connects us with a source of wisdom and knowledge which the logic, structure and over-emphasis on science has cut off from our experience.

Another way that is available to us to tune into our collective unconscious and to benefit from the transmitted wisdom of others is by learning from our dreams. Dreams, according to Carl Jung, are the royal road to the unconscious. They represent the true feelings and desires of the real self. When we dream we are in our most open, honest and expressive state. The defences of the persona are put to one side and our unconscious self is free to tell us what is really going on within. Each dream provides us with a 'right now' picture of what is most important in our lives at this moment. Because we are asleep and our defences are put to one side, the issues that are most pressing in our lives will be free to come out. Because it is our unconscious that is giving this information about ourselves, it is not literal information. The language of the unconscious is symbolic and intuitive and is best interpreted by the creative right side of the brain.

WAYS TO TUNE INTO THE REAL SELF

➤ To learn about the real self it is necessary to acknowledge, accept and integrate the shadow side of the personality.

➤ Being aware of the persona, the needs of our profession, we are able to separate our outer, collective personality from our inner, actual, individual personality.

➤ In getting to know the real self it helps to become conscious of the requirements which the community put on us in order to be accepted in the community. These are necessary, beneficial requirements from which the person and the community mutually benefit, but they may not be in the best interests of the individual.

➤ In discovering the real self, it is necessary for us to pay attention to our intuition, to listen to what we really think and to honour this whenever possible. Doing this will inevitably bring us into conflict with the collective view and will often be difficult but it will bring us to a deeper level of self-awareness and a greater ability to be ourselves within the requirements of the collective.

➤ Knowing the real self demands that we know our individual strengths, capabilities and limitations. An inflated sense of self comes from having an unrealistic concept of self, that is, having an unrealistic, or too self-centred a view of either our capabilities or our limitations. To assume a realistic concept of self it is necessary to accept and acknowledge how good we are as well as how limited we are. This acknowledgment requires a balance between our need for personal self-worth and society's view of what the reality is, in other words a balance between subjective and objective reality.

➤ Knowing the real self means that we need to be in touch with our feeling side, know our feelings and be able to express outwardly what we feel inwardly.

➤ This is particularly true in regard to those feelings such as anger, jealousy and revenge which are often part of the unconscious basis for our actions. Because these negative feelings are unacceptable in society, and because they are unacceptable to us privately and publicly, it is always difficult for the person to acknowledge their presence. The more we deny them the more influential they are in our behaviour.

➤ Accepting the reality of the other person is also important if we are to get to know the real self. There is a subjective reality which is how I perceive the world from my own point of view. This is a subjective, selfish and egocentric approach to life and it is necessary for our survival. But it is important to be aware that it is only one side of the story. Other-awareness or objective reality is essential to enable us to gain acceptance and to avoid attributing an inflated sense of our importance to ourselves and our own place in the world. Developing other-awareness and a sense of objective reality is integral to the development of the real self.

NEVILLE'S STORY

Neville came to me as a young boy in national school as his mother was concerned that he was having difficulty coping in his world of school, the playground and the street. He was unable to stand up for himself, to answer back or to deal with anything that did not fit into his picture of the world.

Neville's difficulties showed in the following ways:

➤ He was unable to deal with any form of criticism either from his peers or from adults
➤ He became very upset if anything unexpected occurred
➤ He was continually tense and anxious by day
➤ At night he was experiencing continuous nightmares
➤ He had a view of himself as a 'good boy' who was superior to his peers
➤ He would not make a decision without first checking with an adult
➤ He was unable to take risks.

When I first met with Neville he was scared, timid and unable to separate from his mother. Initially, I worked with him around issues of developing trust in others, accepting things that he did not agree with, verbal assertiveness, and developing general self-esteem. This work took the form of

➤ playing together
➤ inventing games that were totally fun, playfully competitive, sometimes had rigid rules and sometimes flexible rules
➤ painting, drawing
➤ making people and stories from play-dough, márla and clay
➤ telling stories through sand play
➤ messing with sand, water and paint
➤ imagining, guessing, symbolising
➤ role playing
➤ verbal challenges.

The purpose of this approach was to allow Neville to develop skills of

➤ accepting another view
➤ trusting someone other than his mother
➤ being able to lose
➤ co-operation

➤ coping with uncertainty
➤ expressing his feelings
➤ playing and relaxing
➤ emotional, physical and verbal assertiveness.

My feeling was that the issues which were underlying Neville's symptoms were at least in some measure projections of issues which his mother had in her own life, and that at some time his progress was going to require his mother to withdraw those projections.

The opportunity to raise this with his mother, Doreen, arose when she became concerned that Neville's development was bringing up issues of separation for her.

Doreen was in her mid-thirties and Neville was the apple of her eye. She idealised him and invested all her emotional energy, intellectual hopes and social ambitions in him. He was intellectually bright, physically handsome and behaviourally perfect and represented all that Doreen would have wanted for herself. She kept him as close as she could to her both physically and emotionally at all times. Neville's natural attempts at separation, through socialising with other children on the street, were frustrated unconsciously by Doreen's continual denigration of their behaviour. Neville developed an aversion to normal boyish rough and tumble, took on his mother's sense of superiority towards his peers and remained close to her. Doreen's fear that Neville would replace her and become attached to his peers manifested itself in not allowing him to walk to school, not allowing him to go to the shop on his own, and expecting him to check with her before attempting anything new. Her fears became his fears and resulted in Neville living out his mother's projected dread of separation.

Doreen's ability to take on these issues was helped by the fact that she could see a difference in Neville, that she wanted to 'help' him and also that she wanted to retain her importance in his life. She accepted that it was possible to allow him to be a part of his own world of friends, peers and schoolmates, and yet retain a healthy closeness to him. It meant, at a conscious level, accepting in others, certain behaviours, attitudes and language that she had previously found difficulty with. It also meant bringing to awareness her own unconscious issues around attachment, dependency and trust in others. This was true in relation to her relationship with Neville and in relation to her own personal life.

3

POWER

·◡

The nature of power, its importance in our lives, the abuse of power in many life situations, and the ways in which it can be a positive force in our lives, is central to our ability to live a life that is satisfying and fruitful. In all aspects of living where we come into contact with other people there is a power struggle, a situation where as individuals we try to ensure that our own sense of self and our own view of ourselves as active agents in our environment are not in any way being diminished. We therefore try to make sure that what we want as a means of satisfying our need for survival is looked after. To do this requires that we do not allow the needs of the other person to dominate and at the same time it means that we have to have a feeling of ownership and legitimate power in our own social and personal environment. Inherent in this ownership and power is an awareness of those around us spatially, socially and emotionally and it means not allowing either the ego or the other to be totally dominant or to be totally lost.

Taking ownership means having the courage to take responsibility when things go wrong, being able to accept that even though we are influenced to behave in a certain way, and there are aspects of our environment such as people and events which impact on our behaviour, it is nevertheless the individual who has the most significant influence on his or her own life.

Taking ownership of our lives refers to two aspects of our experience in our world.

Firstly, we can take ownership in relation to our own actions by accepting that whatever outside influences impact on our behaviour, it is we who are responsible. We need to accept that there are many influences that have a bearing on who we are, how we behave and what we think, but it is essential that within the acceptance of this knowledge we take ultimate responsibility for our own lives.

Secondly, we take ownership of our lives by being able to reject any responsibility, blame or guilt that is being wrongly attributed to us.

Taking responsibility for our lives, our behaviour, and our achievements is a key element in the development and maintenance of self-esteem and a sense of self-worth.

It is often difficult for us to take credit for our achievements and there are many possible reasons for this. We may have come through a family or school system where children were not allowed or encouraged to take credit for or to glory in their own achievements. This can create a negative view of personal achievement and may lead to a situation where as adults we may be more likely to attribute success to luck or to another person or agent rather than ourselves.

If as children or indeed later as adults we have been part of a system where achieving success caused envy and resentment among the other members of the group/family then in the interests of our own self-preservation it might have seemed better in the immediate term to either deny our success, hide it, or attribute it to other members of the group. The more we have had to practise this behaviour, the more normal it seems and the easier it is to react in this way. It also becomes more and more difficult to break out of this circle of self-denigration, as it becomes part of our expected behaviour pattern where others are concerned.

Even more important as regards attribution of credit is being allowed and encouraged and given the opportunity to achieve. Where parents or teachers or other carers have placed low value on their own achievements or have achieved very little in their personal lives, they may feel threatened by the achievements of their children or their pupils and unconsciously deny their children opportunities for achievement and success. This creates an unfamiliarity within the child with what it feels like to succeed and the child never learns the value of success as an incentive to achieve. These negative achievement motivators become internalised and assimilated into the overall life package of individuals as they grow to adulthood and they seek out life situations where achievement and success are absent because they are more comfortable in such situations, and uncomfortable in situations where achievement and success are valued.

Where children are not allowed to achieve by themselves, i.e. the adult always tries to either do it for them or tries to 'help' them with the task, this can lead to a situation where children can never say that they have really achieved something. They will not be able to take all the credit as theirs, and will feel uncomfortable unless someone is there to share the laurels.

This inability to take credit becomes part of their way of being, their way of orienting themselves to the world and their usual way of taking on their environment. In the adult it shows up as reticence, inability to participate in groups, unwillingness to take on challenges and a tendency to criticise people who do well. Such people are uncomfortable with the achievements of others because it brings up their own inadequacies.

A similar barrier to taking responsibility in our own lives is where individuals take on responsibility for wrongdoing or take the blame where it is not deserved. If, as children, they have experienced the scapegoat syndrome where they have been given the blame for anything that goes wrong in the family or in the group, they may develop an over-willingness to take the blame in later life. If the role of scapegoat is assigned to particular individuals in a group on a regular basis, they gradually accept that this is normal, and it becomes an expectation. They will find it difficult to reject blame and may often accept blame where it is not theirs.

Part of the process of taking ownership is having a say in what happens to us, having a say in our lives generally.

Having a say means:
- ➤ feeling that we have an opinion
- ➤ believing that our opinion counts as being valuable
- ➤ being able to express this opinion
- ➤ being able to question and respond to the opinions of others
- ➤ being able to hear and accept the opinions of others
- ➤ being able to let others express opinions with which we don't agree
- ➤ rejecting opinions that are wrongly attributed to us
- ➤ making decisions about our lives
- ➤ allowing others to make decisions about their lives
- ➤ questioning decisions that we feel are wrong
- ➤ insisting on being included in decision-making.

For many people, life is a continual process of others making decisions for them, of not having a say in the workplace, in the home, or in any aspect of their lives. This form of passivity, subservience and total powerlessness is often seen in the following situations:

- ➤ In a family situation one or other adult is in total control of the finances. This may begin as a 'normal' situation where one partner is the earner, the person who undertakes what is essentially the traditionally 'masculine' role of the provider. Such a role of itself confers power, control and ownership within the family group in a legitimate and acceptable way, but can become authoritarian rather than authoritative. The transformation from legitimate to abusive power will happen through the interaction of two factors: the desire of one partner to expedite the masculine role of providing for his family and at the same time the willingness of the other partner to be accepting of this. It is the over-development of these legitimate roles that leads on the one hand to abusive control and on the other to abusive passivity. The abusive masculine role is not always carried out by the male partner nor is the abusive passive role always in the female partner. Both partners may become habituated to the 'powerful' and 'powerless' roles and unconsciously begin to accept this as normal.

➤ The same type of situation may arise in the workplace where the person in whom legitimate authority is invested may either consciously or unconsciously abuse this authority. It will be experienced as taking decisions without consultation, putting unreasonable pressure on colleagues to carry out tasks, insisting on unreasonable tasks being done or blaming particular employees when things go wrong.

➤ This type of abuse of power or bullying behaviour has many aspects and it is the result of a combination of factors. Individuals in the position of legitimate power and authority feel threatened by the capability or the achievements of the others in the group. They may be unable to relate to them on an equal basis and in order for them to protect their own view of themselves they believe it is necessary to diminish the others in the group to a point where they feel in control of them. Such individuals are acting out of a low self-image and feelings of inadequacy, in the spurious belief that if they diminish the others sufficiently, everyone will be equal, and they will then be able to handle it. Hand in hand with this is the willingness of the others in the group to accept it. This starts out as a legitimate acceptance of authority and a conditioning to accept the legitimate power of the 'boss'. Both gradually accept the 'normality' of their position and become habituated to their perception of themselves, which makes it so difficult to change.

The lack of say in our lives has important consequences, even if we do not recognise it.

➤ It means a continuous undercurrent of unease and dissatisfaction, without being able to pinpoint the reasons for these feelings. Chronic unhappiness or a sense of there being something wrong within us, breeds anger and resentment, although it may never be constellated at a conscious level. Such anger and resentment is all the more difficult to deal with because the reason for it is hidden.

➤ If we do not have a say in our lives it means that we can never take credit for our achievements, because we will tend to attribute success to those who control our lives, to luck or to some other external factor. This results in a continued lack of a sense of self-worth and prevents the development of a willingness to try, a characteristic that is crucial to achievement motivation.

➤ By handing control of our lives to others we are unable to develop the confidence to fail, a characteristic that is essential to achievement satisfaction, motivation and the sense of usefulness which comes from knowing what we can do. The confidence to fail is essential in developing a willingness to try, while at the same time enabling us to have a realistic concept of self.

➤ If we lack the confidence to take ownership of our lives we will often resort to 'getting others' to do it for us. This is a negative form of power and control and leads to deriving satisfaction from controlling others. It becomes manipulation and bullying and it means that the person is never able to have the satisfaction that goes with knowing he or she can do something and the sense of achievement that accompanies this feeling. Getting someone else to do it for us can be accomplished by overtly and consciously forcing the other person to do what we want. It can be just as successfully done by regressing into the vulnerable helpless role of the child, or it can be done by making others feel bad or guilty if they are unwilling to give us what we want. The inherent danger in this type of powerful powerlessness is that we become comfortable in the role of getting our own way through helpless vulnerability, and are afraid to venture out into the world of personal responsibility.

But taking ownership of our lives also involves taking ownership of our flaws, our negative behaviour, and our positive behaviour.

It is only when we acknowledge, accept and integrate our shadow side into our overall personality that we can make a start on the real business of becoming a whole person.

As we see so often in all individual behaviour we appear to have an inbuilt facility to avoid our faults. There are good reasons for this. To begin with it is often perceived to be too damaging and too painful for us to accept our own negative side. It is much easier to see it in others and when we blame others for 'starting it first' we know that they have learned this from good teachers. The tendency to project our negative side on to others and to blame others for starting it first is part of our way of defending ourselves from the discomfort of seeing our own flaws. Added to this is the societal pressure to be good, to fit in with the persona that society has ordained for us. This demand for conventional moral, social, and emotional standards is brought about through the influence of the family, the school, the church and society in general. The benefits are that it creates an environment where moral and behavioural standards are maintained, and generally makes our world a better place. The difficulty arises where individuals are unable to maintain these standards and find themselves isolated and separated from the main body of society. This acts as a barrier to acknowledging the negative aspects of ourselves because anger and resentment get in the way of our self-awareness.

So, as well as internal pressure not to accept our negative side, there is environmental pressure as well.

The effects of not taking ownership of our shadow side are manifold. If we do not take ownership of the negative side of our being, it means that we are living in an unreal world. We are presenting an unbalanced and incomplete version of ourselves to the world. In addition there is an undeclared secret which we are afraid to disclose to the world. By not taking ownership of the shameful and embarrassing part of ourselves we are living in the pretend world of the persona where we are not fully ourselves but living the life that others set out for us.

➤ In taking ownership of our lives we need to develop a certain amount of self-awareness and self-knowledge.

➤ We are who we are, and accepting who we are, the good and the bad, is essential if we are to take ownership of our lives.

➤ We must learn to accept praise and credit for our achievements. A difficulty in Irish family life and in our school system is the tendency not to praise and not to allow children to celebrate achievements. This can become internalised in individuals and it can become part of people's make-up causing them to be 'unable' to accept credit and possibly attributing their own success to the efforts of others in their lives.

➤ Ownership of our lives also means accepting 'blame' where it is appropriate. Part of our psychological survival kit is an ability to see ourselves as powerful and right and good and where this tendency is allowed to have too much influence in our overall psychological make-up through our own lack of self-awareness, our lack of consciousness of our limitations, we often find it unacceptable to accept the blame for our negative behaviour.

➤ Being able to reject undeserved blame is an important part of owning one's life and all its implications.

➤ In order to take ownership of our lives we have to be able to allow others to take ownership of their lives. This means being able to allow others, our children, partners, colleagues etc to take credit and blame where it is rightfully theirs and also to allow others to have a say in decision-making.

➤ Owning our lives is akin to establishing a psychological, emotional, social, intellectual and physical space in our world. We need to be proud of this space and willing to defend it and at the same time be able to allow others into it without feeling threatened. This pride in our space is essential in order to show those around us that we value it and that we own it, but that we are not overly protective of it and not threatened by the nearness or presence of others. If we value our space in a healthy way it sends out a signal that it is worth valuing and therefore others are more likely to value it.

➤ There is an essential symbiosis between owning our space and allowing others to own their space. It is this respect for space that is the basic principle underlying our ability to form and maintain relationships in the family, in the workplace and in our social lives.

➤ Owning our lives also means taking responsibility for what we say, and being willing to hear what others say. It means being able to acknowledge any wrong or hurtful things that we say and being able to hear the apologies of others.

CAROL'S STORY

Carol is a middle-aged woman, now living apart from her husband. She has four children, and she is making a new life for herself.

Carol grew up in rural Ireland in the 1960s, was a success at school and went to college where she qualified. She married in her early twenties and gave up her job to work in the home. From the time of her marriage she began to experience continued verbal and behavioural abuse. The abusive behaviour continued for twenty years and was in some part facilitated by the fact that Carol was devoted to her children, had a very strong religious faith and believed very strongly in the integrity of the family. An important aspect of Carol's story is that these three factors were more important to her than her own well-being and happiness. She felt that if she looked after her children, her religious practice and her family, everything else would be taken care of. It was the fact that she always put herself second to these other important issues that made it easy for the abuse to happen. These factors, allied to her husband's desire to control her and to keep her submissive, contributed to both the gravity and the extent of the abusive behaviour.

Ownership of the abuse was an important issue. While allowing Carol to see that she herself was a part of the overall picture, she had to know that she could in no way be held responsible for it. The abuse was the property, the work of the person she was married to. Since her husband, John, was unwilling/unable to take part in the work we were doing it was important to examine the issues that were operating for him, the possible reasons for the abuse. Allowing Carol to see that she was part of the overall abusive relationship was important because it enabled her to name her own behaviour, to own it and from this to be able to change. Carol had to see that being part of the overall picture was not the same as being responsible for the abuse. But she needed to acknowledge that her behaviour was contributing to what was happening to her, to enable her to overcome the passive helplessness which is endemic in the victim role.

It was necessary for Carol to be brought to see me by somebody else, because she was unable to come by herself. She was so defeated by the abuse that she was unable to seek help by herself. She had reached a point of such powerlessness and vulnerability that she was totally immobilised by fear, low self-esteem and the feeling that what was happening was in some way justified. Her energy levels were so low that she was on the point of giving up.

Because she was so emotionally oppressed she had reached a point where there was no desire to do anything, she had lost all interest in the future and had no value on her appearance, her life or anything around her. My first meeting with Carol was a meeting with a helpless child.

In the therapy room, because I was a man, she expected to experience all the same modes of behaviour that had been the norm in her life. She was afraid and untrusting and she needed space to tell her story as she wanted to and when she wanted to. For a number of sessions very little was said. There was tearful silence, an integral part of Carol's story, and it needed to be heard and accepted for what it was. It was the first time in twenty years that she had chosen to be silent. It was her statement of the speechlessness and silence which had been forced on her and which had become her defence against the violence in her life.

Carol's story was a catalogue of continued name-calling, obscene threats, hurtful names and words to put her down, insulting terms and language to make her feel small, and indiscriminate blame for anything that went wrong.

Understanding the mostly unconscious motives which caused her husband to treat her in such a damaging and demeaning way was a helpful part of the work of addressing Carol's situation. It was important because we had to make sure that Carol only claimed ownership of what was rightfully hers, and also that she could openly and definitely attribute to her husband what was rightfully his: the active role in the abusive behaviour.

The underlying issues in the abuse were based on John's emotional immaturity and insecurity. Growing up as a child and as an adolescent he had not separated emotionally from the primary attachment figure in his life, in this case his mother. His emotional development had never been exposed in the emotional market place, and he had never had the opportunity to take his chances in relationships because his mother was always there as a safety net. Consequently as far as the emotional side was concerned he remained at an infantile stage.

Marriage merely represented a transfer of this primary attachment from one figure in his life to another. This meant that he expected to have total control over the woman in his life, and that the relationship was not based on mutual emotional satisfaction but on a totally selfish need for satisfaction. His wife became an object which he tried to control and have near him at all times. He could not allow her any independence either socially, intellectually or personally. Marriage in rural Ireland to a person such as Carol provided the ideal growth conditions for this type of abuse.

He chose language as the means of control because this was Carol's most vulnerable place. This was so because of her deep religious faith and because of her need to put her family before herself.

It is important in the wider sense to acknowledge that John was unhappy, depressed and to some extent unconscious of what he was doing. But it was more important still that this was not allowed to divert any attribution, responsibility or will to succeed from the work we were doing. In other words this was about Carol and she needed to know and to feel that it was about her, her well-being and her future right to life. Her husband's role, his responsibility, his feelings about what happened or what was about to happen in Carol's life were not going to prevent her from getting her life back.

In a way it was the synchronistic meeting of John's particular set of emotional and personal needs with Carol's particular vulnerability, each coming from their own particular set of conditions, which ensured that Carol was the victim of a life-long litany of abuse and bullying.

In addressing with Carol the issues involved in the abuse it was important to recognise a number of factors:

➤ Carol had to own her own behaviour.
➤ Her husband's behaviour was his own and Carol could not be responsible for it.
➤ He would not stop just because she wanted him to.
➤ The basis of her husband's abuse was probably an unconscious motive to control and have power over her, based on an infantile fear of abandonment. In other words he did not want to lose her because he thought he could not survive on his own.
➤ Carol had to learn skills of verbal assertiveness and emotional abrasiveness which up to now she would have felt were wrong and which did not sit easily with her view of herself as she previously saw herself.
➤ During the therapy she was going to have to resist John's resentment at losing her in the emotional sense because she was challenging his power over her, and therefore moving out from his sphere of influence. She had to re-evaluate, reconstruct and re-establish her view of masculinity and femininity and of her 'self', within those two ideas.

Carol's work with me was about trust, learning new skills, and confronting her own shadow.

In developing trust there were a number of important issues. The fact that I am a man was important in the overall process of restoring trust, because at this point she believed that all men behaved like John. Creating a safe and non-judgemental space in the therapy room was essential to develop Carol's ego strength. In enabling her to do, and say, and be, in the safety of the therapy room she was able to develop a sense of her own power.

Carol's shadow or weak spot was in a way connected to her goodness as a person. She was vulnerable to the abuse because she believed so strongly in the importance of her role as mother and wife, the integrity of her family and the sacredness of her marriage. What she lacked was the ability to engage in what we might term the rough and tumble of the emotional playground which is characteristic of a healthy, close relationship. Carol's upbringing, her religious background, her respect for the integrity of the family all made it difficult for her to hear bad language. It was even more difficult for her to contemplate using it. So her shadow was in effect really her goodness.

Our work together focused on getting rid of her aversion to this type of abusive language, to take away her fear of the tool of the abuse, which was the language. We addressed this by disempowering the words, by discussing their meaning, and by taking away the emotional resonances from the insults, the obscene language and the swear words that were being used. We continued this by writing them on a flip chart where we could see them and drawing pictures where we could. Eventually we began to use them.

Though the abuse was coming from John it was important that Carol did not see him as the problem. One of the issues we addressed was the need to undemonise her husband. It was important that Carol saw the solution to her problem as being within herself and that whatever John did had nothing to do with how well she did. This was an essential requirement in enabling Carol to regain her personal power. She had to know that it was in her all the time, and that all she had to do was release it. If we focused on John's behaviour we would be putting the solution into his world and taking it away from Carol. Carol needed to feel and to work on the basis that the solution to her problem was within her.

The turning point came when she took the gamble of confronting John and rejecting his abuse. She did this in two ways. Firstly, both inwardly and outwardly she 'refused to accept' the abuse that he was putting on to her. Her refusal to accept was expressed in these ways:

➤ telling herself that it was not for her
➤ putting up a strong psychic barrier between herself and John when he tried to verbally abuse her
➤ verbally rejecting what he was saying
➤ physically rejecting by walking away.

The second part was to 'give it back' to him. This she did by retaliating to show that she was not afraid of the abuse any more.

As in all situations when people learn a new skill, they may feel awkward and ungainly in its use. Carol was no different and she felt unsure and shy and guilty about using the type of language that up to now she had considered to be bad. But the feeling of power afterwards was so strong and so positive and so energising that it overcame any residual guilt or fear that she had.

There was no going back.

4

SURVIVING IN
A GROUP

·‿

Life for the most part is a social activity and this means that in order to live in a holistic way much of our time is spent within a group – the family, the work place, the community or the team. Our ability to function within the group is crucial to our psychological well-being. Each of us has a deep need to belong to a group, to be with other people and to experience the warmth of belonging. We are born into a social setting with an inherited need for social contact and inclusion. This need is heightened by the separation trauma of birth. The emotional resonances of separation trauma are always present in the unconscious and act as a motive for involvement, connection and social interaction.

In this chapter we look at how our efficacy as group members is dependent on our personal, individual capacity to adapt, accommodate and promote ourselves in the emotional cut and thrust of the group. We address some of the issues connected with the formation of groups, the maintenance of their integrity, the difficulties of gaining entry into a group and surviving within the group; we also examine issues such as scapegoating and bullying.

All groups are made up of individuals, all separate and in all cases pursuing their own private agenda of surviving. The healthy tension between the individual and the group is ever-present and though successful groups are those where individuals seem to put the well-being of the group before their own individual well-being, the group will not function as effectively if the individual is totally subsumed by the demands of the group.

In addition to individuals having their own personal survival agenda the group will already have a group behaviour pattern, which has evolved as the group's own particular way of surviving. This will be influenced or changed in some way when a new member joins. The conditions surrounding the new member's entry to the group will determine whether it is the existing group or the incoming individual suffers the most change. When the new member has joined a new pattern of group behaviour will develop which will either include the new member in a positive belonging way or not. A key issue in the happiness of the individual and in the happiness of the group is how well the personal and the collective motives are in recognition of each other and therefore in harmony.

In some cases we choose to become members of a particular group such as a club, a team or the workplace. However, in many cases we find ourselves in a group that we did not choose to join and that may not be meeting our needs. The family is one such group, where the child is part of a group that he or she did not choose, and that sees the child's needs, at least while the child is very young, through the eyes of others in the group.

THE FAMILY

The family is the first group experience for all of us and our experiences of working in a group will be shaped significantly by the way in which we are able to experience being ourselves within this group. The family is a difficult group to survive in because it has a particular status and is seen as being almost above reproach. It is usually patriarchal in its outlook and asserting oneself is usually frowned upon. The accepted 'way of being' within the family grouping is one of passive acceptance of the status quo where any questioning or challenging of the accepted value systems is usually seen as wrong. This has the effect of creating an attitude of acceptance rather than of challenging; an attitude of going along with the group rather than of questioning, and an attitude of accepting the received wisdom rather than of expressing an opinion that appears to go against the group norm.

THE SCHOOL

School is the first group that most people experience outside the family. It represents the first tentative steps towards independence from the protection and dependence of the family. It has separation and attachment issues for both the child going to school and the parent of the child. But the skills required for personal survival within the group of the school are just as diverse and just as important as those required in other groups. There are two important factors at work in this group. Firstly the pressure to conform to the group norm is far greater than in other groups and it is generally accepted that 'everybody' wants the child to conform to the expectations of the school group. These are deemed to be the values attitudes and behaviours which society wants to be passed on. It is very easy for the individual needs of the child to lose out to the collective needs of the school. The second factor at work here is that, while the child is coming from another group where he or she was treated as a special member, the ethos of the school will be to treat everyone the same. Many children are not equipped to survive emotionally in a group where the group is more important than the individual.

THE WORKPLACE

The other group that plays a major part in the life of the individual person is the workplace group of people which we join partly by choice and partly out of a need for survival. This group is not joined for the purpose of satisfying social and belonging needs but because it satisfies our need to provide, our need to achieve and our need for self-promotion. It is through our work that we receive the emotional and material feedback that tells us we are useful to ourselves, to our families and to society. This emotional feedback is the fuel of motivation that gives us the energy to plan for the future, to get up each morning, and to make the effort when things are difficult. It is one of the main ways in which we sustain our life energy.

THE PLAY GROUP

The other significant group for most people is the social group – the sports club, the football team, or the golf club. We join this group because it satisfies our need to belong, our need for affirmation, and our need for fun. In many cases membership of the social group may not satisfy these needs because the team is too competitive, or because the club is too orientated towards business, or because we find that we do not 'get on' with some of the members.

GROUP DYNAMICS

If we watch a group of children playing in a playground when they are on their own and unsupervised, we notice the way in which the rules of joining, being part of, and being thrown out of groups operates. This is the model for the way in which adults conduct the business of groups and clubs and to some extent families.

The family is unique in that we are welcomed into it purely on the basis of our being. We do not have to meet any criteria of shape, size, or ability, and merely by being there we are made to feel welcome. Where in extreme circumstances the child is rejected by the family it is the result of circumstances that are not usual and are due to some serious family difficulty. For the most part we do not have to pass a test to gain full entry to our family. However, this is not the case in terms of remaining an accepted member of the group. The difficulty arises because of the normal healthy and necessary need within each of us to separate from the family. This is part of the growing process and is necessary if we are to become whole beings, able to survive on our own, as emotionally effective persons.

How to balance this healthy need to separate with the equally important need to belong, to be part of a safe group and to feel that no matter what happens we have a safe place to go is a balancing act that causes much difficulty for both individuals and families. The underlying difficulty here is that as a rule society holds the view that if we do not follow the rules of the club, the group or the party then we do not belong within that group. This principle is often seen in the so-called 'tough love' concept where members of a family who break the rules within the family, who persist in behaviour that is unacceptable to the family, are asked to leave or are actually put out. People also become isolated from the family when their way of being, their way of living, their attitudes and ideas do not match those of the family. Even for adults, perhaps particularly for adults, the feeling of being isolated from the first and most important emotional resource that they have ever been a part of, is one of the most destabilising they will ever experience.

Similar patterns of behaviour and group dynamics occur in the workplace. When a new member of staff joins a group for the first time there is a change in the dynamics of the existing group. To begin with, the configuration of the group has changed, the psychic contents of the group have changed and the physical and emotional balance of the group has changed. Some people in the group may feel threatened by the new arrival and this may manifest itself in excessive welcoming of the person into the staff-room, while at the same time the undercurrent is of unease, insecurity and mistrust. In such a situation the new arrival will almost certainly pick up the unconscious negative transference but be unable to explain it. The new arrival may bring skills and expertise and attitudes which some of the established members of staff may not have. Situations such as these make it difficult for a newcomer in a group and demand a strong belief in one's own capabilities. The new member of staff may be a woman entering a predominantly male establishment and gender issues as well as issues of merit and personal insecurity may surface.

Unwittingly or unconsciously we can allow ourselves to become the silent members of the group. This process can originate where people are by nature introverted and acquire the reputation of having very little to say. It may be as quiet, passive and co-operative individuals that they have been accepted into the group, and as they grow, or as they become more accepted members of the group, they themselves begin to believe what the others members of the group think of them. Part of the unspoken agreement between the 'quiet' members and the group as a whole may be that the more they live out the group's perception of them as being quiet, the more accepted they are by the group. So 'quiet' members of the group are rewarded, by having their need to belong fulfilled, for the behaviour which is damaging to them as individuals.

The combined effect of the expectation of the other members of the group and the gradual growing into the role of silent passivity creates pressure both from within and without to be silent and unheard and therefore helpless. In other words it becomes the accepted practice within the group. What happens in situations of learned helplessness is that the person derives power from the helplessness. This process can occur in the family, in the workplace, in society generally or wherever groups operate.

There is however a spurious and damaging power associated with this acquired vulnerability. It comes from the fact that the vulnerable individuals are able, both consciously and uncon-sciously, to engender the sympathy of those around them. The people with the power and those who are silent are comfortable because their needs are being satisfied. The people who are quiet and helpless are satisfying their power needs and their need to belong by acting out the role of the helpless, vulnerable, unassertive member of the group. Unfortunately this is a spurious power and acceptance, and it does not really meet the needs of individuals in a deep and lasting sense. The people who have the power in the situation, the parents, the established members of the group, or the people in authority are satisfied because the quiet members are not challenging their status. So there is a collusion which perpetuates the silence of learned helplessness.

SCAPEGOATS AND STARS

Groups by their very make-up are susceptible to abuse. Because a group is made up of individuals who are inherently different, with different abilities, different psychological make-up, different emotional strengths, and different capabilities in terms of having their needs met, it is inevitable that some of the group members will lose out in the process of meeting their social, emotional and achievement survival needs.

Among the most noteworthy ways in which individuals lose out in the group are through scapegoating and starring, two processes that occur in all groups to some degree. Both occur for the most part unconsciously and the group members may not be aware of what is really going on.

Scapegoating refers to the way in which the members of a group unconsciously ascribe all the negative behaviours, ideas and failures of the group to particular individuals. These individuals may be quiet, unassertive and introverted and may be perceived both by the group and by themselves as being the least effective and the least likely to complain. Through their physical and psychological appearance they send an unconscious message to the others that they will accept whatever is attributed to them. In a perverted way both the scapegoaters and those scapegoated gain satisfaction from this process. The main body of the group feels satisfied, righteous and good, knowing that others are responsible for the mistakes and wrongdoing in the workplace. The scapegoated are 'satisfied' because they feel popular, and even though it is a negative importance they feel that they are valuable to the group.

The family is a more readymade setting for scapegoating. It is a more closed environment, it has an almost religious right to secrecy, and it has an inherent right to adopt an autocratic approach within the boundary of the family. The child who is most likely to end up as the scapegoat in the family is:

➤ not the first born
➤ an introverted personality
➤ a boy who is sensitive and intuitive
➤ a child who through lack of self-esteem always tries to please others

➤ a child who is a maverick and whose orientation to the world differs markedly from the family orientation
➤ a rebellious child
➤ a child who stands out in terms of appearance, ability or needs.

One of the most damaging aspects of scapegoating is that those who are the scapegoats grow into the role, become unable to break out of it because of its familiarity and are afraid to change what they see as their accepted way of behaving in groups. They have learned how to play the role, how to behave in it, and may feel anxious about changing what they are familiar with. As a result, children who are scapegoated are likely to carry into adulthood the expectation, the self-perception and the behaviour patterns associated with being a scapegoat.

Each group, be it the family, the staff, or the team, will also have a star. In a similar way to how the system of scapegoating is established within the group, the star is also developed as a result of the interaction of a particular individual and a particular group. The person who is the star in one group may not be allowed to become the star in another because the second group brings different behaviours and attitudes and a different group survival pattern. Stars have control of the group because they have excessive influence either in a positive or negative way. This may be because they have more intellectual ability, are more physically attractive or are the good boys or girls who always do what they are told. Members of the group defer to them and expect them to behave in a certain way and they in turn confirm these expectations. In the end they become the bullies in the group. They have too much control within the group, the other members collude in their dominance and expect them to behave in this way, and they are trapped in a situation where their own self-view will not allow them to escape and to share the power. In addition they feel they would be unable to cope in a relationship where they have to compete on equal terms, and will only survive where they feel they are in control.

Neither scapegoats nor stars can escape from their negative power without the help of outside intervention.

SURVIVING IN A GROUP

Surviving in a group requires a contract between the group and each individual in it so that all the members can function as individuals in their own right, while at the same time playing a part as members of the group. This is not a written contract or indeed a formal verbal contract. It is a mixture of awareness of each person's own behaviour, an awareness of the other person's space and needs, and a willingness by individual members of the group to bring to consciousness aspects of their own behaviour that they usually prefer to hide. As well as individuals having to do this, there needs to be a conscious recognition by the group of its psychic contents, its needs and its motives.

BE YOURSELF

To survive in a group situation it is important that we survive by being who we are and not by having to engage in behaviour that is not true to our real selves. If we try to survive by taking on a false identity we are building a set of expectations for ourselves that we will not be able to live up to, and this will lead to a continued sense of dissatisfaction with ourselves, lack of achievement motivation, lack of hope and even depression. Survival on the basis of our real selves is about being aware of who we are, who we want to be, being accepting of that and presenting that identity to the group. If we survive on the basis of the false self, by being the domineering star or by being the passive scapegoat, it is survival by spurious power and is damaging to the real self.

HAVE YOUR SAY

To be a healthy member of a group, whether it is the family, the staff, or any social grouping, it is crucial to feel that you have your say, that you are able to say what you feel and that you take the chance to say it. Not having your say can be caused by the force of the group not allowing you to do so in a bullying, dismissive way. But it can also be because you feel that you do not have anything worthwhile to say, that you are not important enough to be heard, and that you appear to the group as a person who does not usually have anything to say. Not having your say leads to frustration, resentment and feelings of powerlessness, as well as depriving you of any input to what is happening in the group.

The following are effective strategies for changing a situation where you have no say:

➤ Before any change is possible there has to be awareness of what is wrong, acknowledgement of the problem and ownership of each person's behaviour in the situation. Taking ownership is a crucial element in dealing with behaviour change.

➤ Practise, on your own if necessary, saying what comes into your mind.

➤ Allow others the space and the permission to have their say, and hear what they have to say.

➤ Separate what others say from who they are or what you think of them. It is very easy to attribute our feelings about a person to the things he or she says, and because of this never really know what the other person has said.

➤ Accept justified criticism no matter how difficult it is for you.

➤ What you say is not wrong but it may not be acceptable to others.

➤ What you say is not 'you'. It is merely what you think. When you are about to say something that you think will be unpopular, or when you say something that is unacceptable to the group, it is important to see this as just one element in the whole you.

➤ Most good ideas start off being 'wrong', and in accepting that what you have to say can be 'wrong', you are beginning the process of development and growth.

➤ 'Just say it.'

➤ Know your needs.

Changing the dysfunctional group/family situation is as much about the way the group treats individuals as it is about how people behave in relation to their own needs both as individuals and as members of the group. It is important that we know our own needs and are willing to express them in the context of the group without feeling guilty about it. The way we present ourselves to others has a significant effect on the way others treat us and if we present to others as diffident and apologetic, we are less likely to have our needs met. If we are diffident and apologetic this transmits to those around us as 'my needs are not really that important to me, and it doesn't matter if I have them met or not'.

BE A MEMBER OF THE GROUP

If we take a back seat in the group and do not contribute to discussions, decisions and tasks we create a predisposition to being left out. Even though we may contribute to our being left out, and at a conscious level we may accept it, being left out still affects us. Unconsciously we feel resentful, not needed and isolated and while this remains unconscious, our anger is internalised and turned on to ourselves. This further alienates us from the group and in a sense confirms our view that we have nothing to contribute. Breaking out of this requires us to take risks, to exaggerate participation and to overdo our contribution to the activities of the group until we accept ourselves as members of the group. In short it requires us to break out of our own stereotypical view of ourselves.

SEPARATE THE PERSON FROM THE PERSONA

In the workplace, we are usually very taken up with the job we do, the perceived acceptable behaviour and dress for that job, the perceived correct way of being in relation to the boss, our colleagues and our attitudes to work practices. This is a necessary living in the persona which enables us to survive in a way that fits in with our self-view. However, though the persona may be dominant and over-evident in the workplace, it does not mean that there is not a person underneath it. Difficulties experienced as an active participant in the group within the workplace can be persona-based or they can be personal, but if we fail to look underneath the persona we may become stuck in an emotional cul de sac. We find we are unable to move forward because we see only part of the problem. Every persona has a person underneath. The persona is our outer mask, our agreement to abide by certain conventions so that we can be accepted as part of the collective. Though it is mostly the persona that manifests itself in the workplace it is important that individuals are able to display the human feeling and creative aspects of their personality while at work. There can be a fear that if we show too much of our real selves it will make us more vulnerable to those around us and we will lose out in the promotion stakes. So it is the ability to take the emotional risk in the company of our colleagues that can pay the dividend.

ACCEPT YOUR LIMITS

Working and living in a group changes the behaviour of individuals. In a group we feel under scrutiny, under more pressure to perform and for most of us less sure of how good we are. We become more influenced by what others think of us and it can be difficult to resist the temptation to show off by attempting things that are beyond our capability. It is a very strong statement of being human and of wanting to be a part of something when we admit that we have limits. As well as an invitation to the group to 'join with me', admitting our limits takes away unnecessary pressure to perform.

KNOW YOUR STRENGTHS

Just as important is knowing, accepting and owning your strong points. Perhaps there is a cultural predisposition to hide our talents or perhaps it is rooted in a fear that they will not be good enough, which makes us want to keep them to ourselves. By accepting our good points openly and without any coyness we are sending a message that we believe in ourselves and are happy to let them see who we are. This makes the other members of the group more accepting of us.

OWN YOUR OWN BEHAVIOUR

One of the most difficult things for people to do is to accept ownership of their behaviour. This inability to accept that 'I did this', that 'I am responsible for that', that 'I caused this to happen' is more prevalent when it is negative behaviour that is in question. The responsibility of the group is to create an open, blame-free environment where it is possible for the individuals in the group to accept their mistakes. The challenge for the person in this situation is to take the chance on losing group approval, in acknowledging his or her negative behaviour. One of the helpful aspects of this is that by admitting our fallibility, by acknowledging our weakness, we are making it easier for the group to include us.

ENTER INTO THE COLLECTIVE SPIRIT

One of the main ways in which people get left out of groups is, if the group as a whole feels that a particular individual is not committed to the collective value, does not support the group ethic, does not contribute to the achievement goals of the group and does not try to become involved in group activities. This behaviour can transmit itself to the group as the individual rejecting the group. The group, be it a family or a club or a staff, feels that its integrity and existence as an entity is under threat. Where this happens, the group engages in its own way of ensuring its survival, by putting legitimate pressure on the individual to conform to the group norms. This is reasonable and is a useful social behaviour modifier.

For individuals it is possible to subscribe to the group need without losing their identity. Surviving in a group means two things: that the individual people who constitute the group should be able to survive with their personal integrity intact and that the group should not be at the mercy of any one individual. If the group is dysfunctional then all the members are in some way affected by this and if any one member is outside the integrity of the group then the whole group is in some way diminished by this.

MARTIN'S STORY

Martin works in an office with a small group of professional people. For many years he has felt excluded, undervalued and unheard. At the moment he feels that he is being bullied by one other member of the staff. He feels that this person is isolating him, not hearing him, verbally bullying him and devaluing his contribution to the collective effort. Martin at the moment feels that not only is he being bullied, but that the whole staff are in collusion with the person bullying him and are against him.

The person accused, Áine, feels that the allegations made by Martin are not true and that she is being unfairly targeted. There is pressure on this person to accept that the allegations are true and there is a need for the person being bullied to be vindicated.

The other members of the group do not want to be involved and are trying to stay out of it. They feel it has nothing to do with them and they naturally don't want to become part of the negative damaging transference that exists between Martin and Áine.

This case shows the way in which bullying has an unconscious dimension to it and it shows how the group as a whole is contaminated by the psychic contents of one or more of its constituent members.

Before there were any allegations of bullying it was evident that Martin and Áine did not like each other, did not spend time together unless it was required by their job, and had different personality types. It was evident that there were feelings of anxiety, unease and hostility when they were in the same room together.

Martin is an introverted, intuitive, creative, independent and very self-reliant person who does not like to depend on others for anything. He tends to keep to himself, does not share personal details with colleagues and guards his own personal space. He has high standards of integrity and sometimes feels that these are not shared by others. He will only contribute to group activities and discussions when required to do so and is very conscious of his personal safety when expressing opinions. Martin tends to be protective about how he works and is defensive if asked to share ideas. He generates a sense of vulnerability and helplessness, but is unable to accept support from colleagues, because it signifies weakness on his part.

Áine is strong, assertive and very conscientious about her work. She is gregarious and extroverted and is happy to talk openly about her life and work. She is popular with her colleagues and joins easily in collective activities. One of her strongest points is her sense of belonging to a group and her commitment to the idea of collective responsibility. She expresses her opinions strongly and can take criticism. She has a very strong sense of who she is and has a high sense of self worth. She is well liked by her colleagues and is considered to be a good team player.

The significant aspect of all this is that Martin's shadow is Áine's strong point, or superior function, and Áine's shadow is Martin's strong point. In the reality of everyday life within the work situation, this means that both Martin and Áine are the manifestation of each other's negative aspects. They each see in the other the living embodiment of their inadequacies and shadow. This is the root of their dislike, mistrust and hostility.

The situation between them is made worse because there is projection at work and there is an unconscious need for both of them to see their flaws in the other, and an unconscious satisfaction when they do.

In working with Martin and Áine a number of issues had to be kept in focus:

➤ The fact that Martin felt that something was wrong meant that for him there was something wrong and this had to be held for him. But while his reality was that he was being bullied and this had to be honoured, his reality was not necessarily the reality for Áine. The challenge was to establish an objective reality that contained and protected their personal needs and at the same time provided a space for an intersecting common reality.

➤ Although Martin was the person who complained and therefore had the 'moral advantage' in the situation, it was essential to be able to hold Áine's position.

➤ Working through the process was going to involve working individually with Martin and Áine, working dually with them, and working collectively with the group.

We began by trying to bring to consciousness the unconscious issues which both Martin and Áine had, to allow them to own their behaviour, and to acknowledge the role they themselves were playing in the situation. Later in the process the group would have to do the same thing.

For Martin this was difficult because he felt that he was the wronged party, and as such he felt that the responsibility to admit wrongdoing and to change behaviour was all Áine's. It was essential that Martin had support in this, so that the genuineness of his position and his claims would not be undermined. Achieving the balance between owning his behaviour and allowing him to hold his position of victim was the key to success.

To help with this it was necessary to engage with Martin around issues of self-awareness – how he saw himself and how he felt others saw him. This was very sensitive ground for a person such as Martin who was so protective of his personal space and his inner self. And it was in this area that we began by dealing in an academic way with the whole concept of defence, why it is necessary and what it means when something is defended. By focusing on other areas of human activity such as history, sport, and war we were able to put a context on the issues which Martin could deal with. Because he is an intuitive and creative person, dealing with ideas comes easily to him and this intellectualising helped to approach the question of his own defence in an experiential way. In beginning to look inside himself and by being able to accept what he saw he realised that even the negative, shadow side wasn't so bad after all. In realising that he himself could accept the shadow side of his being he began to believe that others might also be able to accept it, and that he had no need to hide it from the outside world. This was the root of the shadow, that somehow parts of his make-up were so bad that if people found out they would completely reject him. And for Martin the proof of this was that he couldn't accept them himself.

Side by side with this, but separate from it, was the process of working with Áine. For Áine this was just as difficult as it was for Martin because she felt that she was being unfairly accused, and therefore had no case to answer. So working with Áine revolved around allowing her to hold her sense of rightness while at the same time bringing her to a position where she could allow Martin to be where he was. The fact that Áine was popular both as a person and as a colleague made it difficult for her to begin acknowledging her shadow, as she felt that there was no shadow. So this part of the work had to be separated from the whole process of the bullying and seen as her own journey of self-development. At a later stage it was possible for Áine to see Martin as the catalyst in her personal growth in as much as it was through him that her negative aspects were constellated. Approaching the fact that she had a shadow was difficult for Áine but more difficult still was facing up to what this shadow was. As it began to emerge that the qualities she did not like about herself were the very qualities that she did not like in Martin, her resistance to the work strengthened. It was painful for her to realise that she had a negative side but to find that this linked her to Martin made it more difficult to accept.

For both Martin and Áine it was necessary to come to a place where they each could see and accept where the other was at.

Because all the members of the group worked in the same space, inhabited the same psychological and emotional space and because they interacted with each other verbally, physically, emotionally and intellectually, it was not possible to resolve the bullying situation by working with Martin and Áine alone. The group as a whole was 'contaminated' by the transference between the two main participants. Also, there was the relationship of the group with both Martin and Áine, a relationship that was for the most part unconscious and significantly different. In Martin's case the relationship was one of patronising helpfulness, which gave the group considerable power over Martin in as much as he was not being treated as an equal, but was being kept in a position of dependency. This relationship was well-intentioned at the conscious level, but in effect was damaging to both the group and to Martin. It was a co-dependent relationship which was making it easy and comfortable for Martin to remain where he was, but was denying him any impetus to move out of his comfortable victim status. For the group members it was damaging because they were not conferring equality status on Martin and therefore not benefiting from what he had to offer. While Martin was being emotionally stifled by the excessive sympathy of the group, the group itself was being rendered dysfunctional by the fact that Martin was not being allowed to contribute as an equal member.

For Áine, because her normal way of being was close to the group's view of the world, the relationship with the group was one of unconscious support and therefore collusion. This was tantamount to collusion with how Áine felt about Martin, and the group's unconscious message to Áine was, keep it up, you're doing fine. It had the effect of taking away any need for change, or to see things differently.

The group had to be involved in the overall process of healing because as a group it was colluding with both people and was also being affected by what was happening. Most members of the group had difficulty with this idea and felt they were being used to deal with an issue that had nothing to do with them. For the group there were two main issues, inclusion and collusion. We looked at how each member of the group felt about these issues and focused on the fact that the group had taken on its own particular collective feeling towards both Martin and Áine. This collective feeling was separate from what each individual in the group felt, it was unconsciously formed and was not overtly expressed at any time. It was easier for members of the group to accept that they were part of a collective collusion, but it was still important that each person in the group acknowledged and owned his or her individual behaviour in what was happening.

This stage in the process was the opportunity for Martin and Áine to be included in the group as equal members with no special status, either positive or negative.

5

HAVING A SAY

•◞

Many issues arise, in relationships, in groups, in families and in our lives generally, around our ability or inability to communicate. In the normal day-to-day world, situations will continually arise where people are misunderstood, where people feel frustrated because they have not been able or allowed to say what they want, where people at work feel that their point of view or their suggestion has been ignored, or in a marriage where people become angry or silent or aggressive because they failed to say something or because they took the wrong meaning from what was said.

COMMUNICATION

The basic currency of communicating between people is that both parties know what the other is saying, and that the right of each person to have a say is respected. It requires an awareness that each person's reality can be different, and that an objective reality may lie somewhere between the two subjective realities. The ability to say what we mean and the skill to say it in a way that is not threatening is developed over time and much of the difficulty about communicating is related to this.

Having a voice, or being heard, is an essential element in how we see ourselves and how others see us, and in the value that we attach to who we are. Having a voice, saying what we want to say and being heard by others around us, are all integral to self-esteem. Healthy self-esteem means that we will be able to have our say and having our say with others will help to enhance our self-esteem. Much of our feelings of value and worth about ourselves come from what we think others think of us and this is communicated to us through what they say to us and how they say it, and what we feel we can say to them.

Being able to say what we want to say, and feeling that what we have to say is worth saying, that it is worth being heard by those who are listening, is a habit that is established in the family and in the school. The ability to have our say and the feeling of worth that we attach to what we have to say are both closely linked. Of crucial importance in developing the skill of having a say, and the feeling that goes with it, are the experiences we have with our teachers and our parents as we grow. The reactions and responses of the significant others in our lives are crucial in allowing us to feel that what we have to say is valuable, worth saying and worth hearing.

WHAT DO YOU MEAN?

Much of the difficulty around communication arises because of the gap between what we mean to say and what we actually say. This gap exists, to some degree, because of the difference between what we say consciously and what we say unconsciously. We often use the phrase 'I didn't mean to say that.' This is another way of saying that it was an unconscious statement, meaning that we didn't plan to say it or we didn't intend to say it, but we had an unconscious reason for saying it. What we say unconsciously is often much closer to what we really feel than what we say in a considered way. An aside to this is the tendency to measure our words or to take time to think before we speak; this is generally seen as being more acceptable and more desirable than speaking spontaneously.

An example of how the unconscious message is different from what is being consciously transmitted would be as follows. A husband who says, 'Would you like to go out tonight?', might be unconsciously expressing his own desire to go out. He is expressing his conscious desire to take his wife out but at the same time an unconscious wish to satisfy his own desire to go out. He may not be aware of the reason or motive and he may be consciously and overtly saying to his partner that she can have a choice or that he would like to take her out, while at the same time seeking to satisfy his own need to go out.

What we say will often carry a different meaning for the person hearing it than for the person saying it. This discrepancy arises because the person we are speaking to is in 'a different place', has a different agenda and may not be aware of the situation of the person speaking. Where the speaker is a person of higher status than the listener, or where the speaker is afraid of the listener, the signal sent by the speaker may not always be the message received by the listener. This often occurs where a parent or teacher is speaking to a child. The child may not understand the words in the way the adult understands them, the child may be so awed by the adult that he or she fails to hear what is said or the child may be afraid and therefore doesn't assimilate what is said. The same verbal relationship can exist between adults, particularly where there are unconscious issues influencing the speaker or the listener.

HAVE YOUR SAY!

Feeling that we have a say, that what we say matters to the listener, and that what we say counts in the greater scheme of things, is important in enabling us to actually say what we want. Being 'able' to say what we have to say is about having confidence in ourselves and in the listener. It gives us a feeling of legitimate power and a feeling that we matter. If we do not have a say, if we are not allowed to have our say, or if we are unable to say what we want to say for some reason related to ourselves, we will exist in a cocoon of frustration, powerlessness and isolation. This cocoon will become stronger and stronger until it becomes a hard shell from which it is very difficult to escape. As the hard shell of silence becomes stronger and stronger, the person within it becomes habituated to it and loses the need or the courage to break out of it.

The ability to have a say is a function of the overall psychological make-up of the person and depends on a willingness to try and a confidence to fail, all wrapped up as 'I have a say'.

Take, for example, the case of a man in the workplace who, through a combination of his own inability to have a say, and the unwillingness of his colleagues to allow him to have a say, gradually becomes powerless, frustrated and isolated. This begins either because he is shy and unsure, or because the group is overly aggressive and is unwilling to 'let him in'. The perception of this man as one who 'doesn't say very much' grows both in the collective mindset of the group and in his own mind. As the stereotype is formed and confirmed by the man's behaviour and that of the group, he becomes angry and the anger is internalised and turned against himself. It may also be projected on to a member of the group. This anger and hatred not only paralyses him but the group is also affected and cannot work effectively until the issue is resolved.

The resolution of the issue involves all the members of the group being free to have a say, without the fear of upsetting others. It usually means outside intervention to provide a space and 'permission' for everyone to hear and be heard. One of the main obstacles to changing this type of situation is the need in us all to blame and to punish. The persons seen as the reason for the silence are unconsciously given the label of 'bad guys', which makes retribution seem necessary. The solution to this verbal bullying is not to turn the tables but to provide an open, creative and blame-free space where everyone's desire to speak and be heard is honoured.

One of the basic requirements of being able to have a say is to be able to allow the other people in the equation, your workmates, your brothers, your team-mates, your partner, to also have their say. This can be difficult because it requires us to do something that on the surface we don't like doing. It requires us to put the other person in a higher place than we are ourselves, at that moment, and this can feel as if we are putting ourselves down. Practising the art of allowing others to have their say is difficult

because we may be coming from a place where this was not practised and we may be afraid that if we allow others to have their
say it will mean that we will be silenced. So it involves a vote of
confidence in ourselves, a willingness to listen and the courage to
speak up.

Having your say depends on not being afraid of what others
have to say and not being afraid of what you have to say yourself.
It means the courage to hear unpleasant things about yourself,
accepting or rejecting them, and being brave enough to express
unpopular opinions, when necessary.

Having a say empowers people because it allows them to feel
included in decisions, to have a legitimate feeling of power in
their environment, and to feel that they are important and rele-
vant in what is going on.

➤ By being aware of what is going on within our own world,
  what we are really saying, and what is really important to us,
  we will be able to 'know' more clearly what we are saying.
➤ If we ask ourselves the question 'What do I want to say here?,
  and then say it we will have a better chance of having our
  point of view heard.
➤ If we are unsure of what people are saying, or what they mean,
  we can help ourselves and them by asking for clarification. It
  is often difficult, especially in a group, to admit that we don't
  understand, or that we didn't hear because we feel that this will
  damage out status within the group.
➤ We need to be conscious of achieving a balance between
  allowing other people to have their say and not being silenced
  through our own need to please.
➤ A significant factor in being able to communicate with others
  is the feeling of being heard. Over-talking and dominating
  conversations results from the feeling that one is not being
  heard. If the listeners are made to feel that they are being
  listened to, that they are being heard, then they are more
  likely to be able to allow others to have their say.

➤ Being heard and getting our message across is rooted in confidence. How we say it is as important as what we say. A strong, confident tone of voice tells the listeners that we ourselves think it is important, that we want to be heard and that we believe in what we are saying.

➤ When two people are in conversation there is communication at the conscious level and at the unconscious level. The conscious communication is in the form of talking, listening, physical contact or any form of overt behaviour. The unconscious communication refers to those unconscious movements, body language, turning away while talking, shifting uncomfortably in one's chair, lack of eye contact, facial expression, which are part of all interaction.

➤ Silence is one of the most fruitful though unappreciated forms of communication. Like all forms of communication it needs to be learned, practised and developed. Silence allows us to be where we are, it allows other people to be where they are; it allows them to tune into their unconscious levels and discover what is really going on for them, and how they really feel about it. The skill of being silent and allowing others to be silent requires us to be comfortable with our own negative issues. When we sit in silence we become uncomfortable and will try to fill the space with talk. We are uncomfortable with our own thoughts and perhaps with the feeling that our power over the others is diminished, because we don't know what they are thinking.

➤ Argument is a very positive and creative form of communicating. The connotations surrounding arguing are in the main negative, due to the fear that it will take control and lead to violence. It is however one of the ways in which we get our point of view across. It usually involves two people communicating in a very feeling and honest way, but the underlying negative affect which attaches to the idea of arguing distracts from its value.

Mark's story

Mark is a thirty-five year old man working on a staff of about twenty colleagues, male and female. He is intellectually bright, intuitive and introverted.

In general he is uncomfortable in a crowd and is more at ease in smaller groups, or in one-to-one situations where he will not have to stand out or have the spotlight on him. He is seen by his colleagues as shy, quiet and not having a lot to say. This perception has been formed as a result of the combination of Mark's own behaviour and the resultant expectation of the group.

When the group meets either socially or for work reasons Mark will tend to sit on the fringes or to separate himself from the main body of the group. This unconscious behaviour on Mark's part sends a message to the group that although he is quiet and shy he is in effect setting himself apart from the group and in a way setting himself above the group. The group's response tends to be an unconscious pushing out, a rejection of Mark by their group energy. Mark's already established feeling of isolation and rejection with his colleagues is confirmed.

When the time comes to be heard, to have a say in the group, Mark, who is predisposed to keeping his opinions to himself, has the further difficulty that he now feels the group does not want to hear them and at the same time is unconsciously making it difficult for him to say what he wants.

The result of all this is that Mark becomes angry and frustrated, begins to feel that he doesn't have a say, and that he doesn't count. The anger is usually internalised and turned against himself but may at times be turned on to a member of the group.

When I first met with Mark he was confused about what was going on within himself, scared that there was something seriously wrong with him, and finding it very difficult to cope.

Working with Mark helps to highlight a number of important issues:

➤ It shows us that while problems are invariably rooted in people's environments, e.g. family and place of work, the core issue is within themselves and the solution is also within themselves.

➤ It shows how it is the interaction of people themselves and all that they bring to a situation, with the perceptions, expectations and behaviour of their environment, that leads to the crisis which causes the problem behaviour.

➤ It brings into focus the idea of equalisation in the therapy process.

➤ It also brings into focus the importance of the transference between the therapist and the client, where the therapist and the space within the therapy room become the symbol for the client's outer world.

➤ Finally it helps us to put 'prior upbringing' and 'recovered emotional memory' into perspective.

Though the issue here is linked, as all issues are, to the immediate environment, Mark and I decided to work on the basis of these two principles:

➤ We cannot control others in our lives.

➤ If we want to change the way people treat us one of the most effective ways is to change our own way of being.

The main issues that we decided to work on were

➤ the connection between how he saw himself, how he thought others saw him and the fear he had that people knew about his shadow

➤ being the centre of attention

➤ taking and giving criticism

➤ ownership of what is rightfully his own.

In Mark's case all of these issues were connected and therefore could not be addressed separately. In working with Mark the therapy room was the model for his environment and we used it as a symbol of how his life was and could become. At the start of our work together it was important that the place we were in emotionally and behaviourally reflected and was in sympathy with where Mark was in his own reality. Mark's reality at this stage had to be acknowledged and accepted as 'the' reality, unconditionally. This meant that there could be no sense in the room that his reality was wrong or had to be changed. It is best described as accepting the rightness of his wrong. Though Mark felt that there was something wrong with him and that he wanted to change this, without delay, it was essential that both he and I were able to 'be' where he was. In doing this a number of issues arose. Firstly, Mark's impatience to be 'cured', as he saw it, could become a barrier to progress as it could prevent him from accepting himself as he then was. There was also the risk that I would be seduced by the attraction of the quick fix and the kudos that this would bring.

We overcame this difficulty by working on the basis that there was nothing 'wrong' with Mark any more than there is with any 'ordinary' person and that the difficulties he was experiencing now were real, an actual living part of him, not an external appendage that had been attached artificially. As such we agreed that in some degree these aspects of himself would always be there, though not in a way that would cause him distress. He would change and look at them in a different way and as his ego strength grew he would be able to live with them and accept them. When this happened, and it was important that he believed it would happen, he would be different and therefore would see himself as an integrated whole and not as a person made up of disparate pieces that he could not accept, and that seemed not to be related to each other.

One of the most significant issues that came up during the work with Mark was the importance of prior upbringing and experience in the process of therapy. At the start we agreed that it was Mark as he was now that we were dealing with, and this raised the question of what role his emotional memory would play in the process. We agreed that we could not totally ignore what had happened to him as this would in a way be the same as denying a part of him. So it was important to recall and bring into the secure emotional space of the therapy room all those things that in his recovered memory were important. This was necessary so that he could feel that he was being wholly accepted into the world of the present reality. But this was not the key issue in Mark's story. In acknowledging and honouring what had happened to him, we agreed that we would not attribute blame and that we would not allow the past to block the path to the future.

At the centre of Mark's prior personal experience was a very strong negative mother complex, which manifested itself as a negative dependency. This dependency was characterised by hostility, mistrust and anger towards his mother and it constituted a relationship that was based on issues which should lead to separation rather than connection.

It was as if Mark was imprisoned in a negative relationship that was blocking the creative and connecting energies necessary for him to live 'his' life. This blocking was also important when he was in the process of therapy, because if we became stuck in trying to sort out the negative relationship with his mother, we would become hooked in to the origins of his situation and divert energy away from the issues that were now active in his life. His current issues were shaped by the past issues but they were not the same in either content or structure. Mark had difficulty with the idea that this was his and his alone to deal with. He knew that others had contributed to his 'now' situation and naturally a part of him wanted revenge. More importantly he wanted to help the people who had done this to him. We needed to address this feeling of his moral superiority and his desire to control the others through helping them to do what he was doing. As he saw it, the other members of his family were missing out on the chance to deal with the negative issues in their lives.

It was helpful to work around the question of ownership and to work towards a place where Mark could allow his mother and the other members of his family to own their behaviour and to have the right to their wrongness. This separation of the 'now' and the 'then' was an important part of the progress that Mark was making. He began to see that like everyone in his world he was a function of his past and that this would always be there, but that changing his world was his responsibility, and if he remained stuck in the past he was dealing with what he could not change. He needed to accept that his recovered memory of his upbringing was his, and the acceptance of this in the therapy process meant that it was 'right' as far as the world was concerned, but that it was only his. My acceptance of his rightness, on behalf of the outside world, made it easier for him to accept the rightness of his mother's wrong.

During this time an important aspect of the process emerged. Mark was finding that there were times when we were not in agreement. At first we had to address the question of his fear of my anger, disagreement or criticism. Initially this fear was so strong that it was kept inside and it was a matter of gradually finding out that there was no danger. On occasion we discussed the possibility of consciously 'getting angry' but we agreed that we would not. It was clear that he was not ready to do this. Such continuous consultation was helpful in building confidence and assurance that the negative mother would not come into the therapy room.

A turning point came one day when Mark asked if he could switch roles and 'ask' me some questions. This was an opportunity for him to test me, to challenge me, and to find out who I was. It was an important issue for me professionally as it meant handing over some of my personal life to Mark, but at the same time it would mean that Mark would begin to see me as a person, not as some form of superior expert who had all the answers. This was a sensitive shift as it would also mean that the dependency which was so important in bringing Mark to this point was to change. I took it that as this was Mark's request it was the right thing to do. Symbolically it was the movement from dependent to independent, from passive to active, from mother to Mark.

6

WHOSE ISSUE IS IT ANYWAY?

When a group of people live together, either in a family or in a community, when a group of people work together, or when a group of people play together, as in a team, there is a continuous psychological overlap of contents, both consciously and unconsciously. What this means is that each person is a carrier for some of the ideas, attitudes and issues of the people with whom he or she is in contact. Each person in the family, the group, or the staffroom is at one time or another a carrier for some of the thoughts, ideas and attitudes of others within the group. This happens through a process called transference and is both conscious and unconscious. Neither the person 'receiving' the contents nor the person 'sending' the contents may be aware of the transference.

The more significant the relationship between members of the group, the more influenced they are by the psychological overflow from the others.

The significance of the relationship can be positive or it can be negative. Where a person in a group has a very positive and satisfying relationship with other members of the group or with the group as a whole, there will be a willingness to take on some of the ideas, attitudes and values of this person or group. So the conscious transference will be stronger, but there will also be unconscious transference of contents from one to the other. What is perhaps more significant and more powerful is when there is negative transference within the group. This occurs where there is a negative or hostile relationship between members of the group. Though the negativity may not be expressed openly it will be transferred unconsciously from one to the other. This in turn will lead to the negative transference being assimilated into the psyche of the receiver and the resultant counter-transference will be filtered through this negative view, back to the original. When this happens unconsciously the transference of contents from one person to another takes place without either person realising it, and the influence can therefore be greater. We see this in many situations.

For example, a child lives with his parents, who do not get on very well with each other. He is an only son and the parents have high expectations for him both academically and socially. The child is the only reason that the parents are together. They don't like each other, don't love each other, and feel that they must stay together 'for the sake of the child'. There is continual animosity and competition between the parents and the child picks this up in the following way. Firstly, he sees the overt manifestations of this hostility in arguments, disagreements and fights. Many parents will feel that if they have their fights when the child is in bed or when he is at school, he will not be affected. But the child becomes the conduit through which the parents transmit their feelings about each other. He becomes frightened, as he feels that the anger and hostility is directed at him and that he is the target of his parents' anger. He becomes concerned for his parents, and worried that he is the cause of what is happening. In order to survive in this he withdraws emotionally from his environment. He protects himself from the emotional abuse by shutting himself off in an emotional vacuum where he will be untouched by what is going on around him. This is his way of surviving and maintaining an acceptable level of siding with each of his parents.

His parents are probably unaware of what is causing their child to behave in this way and will seek the answer by trying to 'help' the child.

But it is only by looking at what is going on between themselves, both consciously and unconsciously, that they will see what

issues are causing the tension and negativity that is being transferred through the child.

In the case of a group the same principle applies. Whether it is
a group who work together, a group who socialise together or a
group who live together as in a family, the psychic contents of
each member will overlap into the psychological world of the
others and the collective contents will be shared. This means that
all the members of the group are affected when there is antipathy
or hostility between any other members of the group. It may only
actively involve two members of the group, but because there is a
collective psychic world which all the members inhabit, and
because each member is connected to the other's psychological
world, what is going on for any individual member of the group
has significance for all the group.

This transference has particular relevance where bullying occurs
in the workplace or in the family. In many cases one person in
particular is bullying another, and solutions may well focus on the
two active parties in the conflict. But it is crucial in such conflict
situations that consideration is given to the collective issues. The
people who are apparently uninvolved in the conflict will have
been drawn in and may be colluding or even actively supporting
or opposing one side or the other.

Because all the members of the group interact with each other
and depend on each other, there is a constant overlapping of
contents from one to the other. This applies to all members of the
group and some aspects, feelings, attitudes and prejudices will
percolate from the two active participants in the dispute. In effect
all the members of the group will unconsciously take in some of
the emotional attachments of the 'protagonists' in the dispute, and
will therefore be more sympathetic to one side or the other.

In addressing such conflict situations it is necessary to take into
account the fact that all the members of the group are in some way
involved and affected by what is happening. It is only by engaging with all the members of the group, be it a staff, a family, or a
team, that a complete resolution can be achieved. Including all the

members of the group in the 'treatment' has many effects:

➤ It acknowledges the role of all the members of the group.
➤ It lessens the sense of isolation and the 'singling out' of any one member of the group.
➤ It creates a sense of inclusion and belonging by sharing the responsibility of dealing with the problem.
➤ It ensures that all the residue and psychological overflow or transference is dealt with and it also taps into the resources of all the members of the group.

ROBERT'S STORY

My first contact with the family was a request to help Robert's son, Kieran, an adolescent boy who was being bullied at school. The request came through the mother who was very distressed, upset and worried. When she was telling her story it was evident from the depth of her emotional connection to her son's experiences that it was more than just her son who was being bullied.

Kieran came to see me with his mother, one afternoon, and presented as a deeply sincere, naïve and unsure young man. He readily connected with the accepting and creative space of the therapy room, and had no difficulty in telling his story.

Kieran's was a story of continual rejection, isolation, loneliness and feeling put down. At the start of his work with me all this was within the context of school, and as far as Kieran was concerned, school was where the problem existed. His peers at school were causing the problem and this was confirmed for him by the fact that his parents tried to help him by addressing the issues with the school. When the taunting and humiliating behaviour became too much for him to cope with he would then resort to violent and aggressive retaliation. This often resulted in suspension from school which was, in Kieran's world, a continuation of the rejection and isolation that he was already experiencing with his peers.

His sense of worthlessness was added to at home where his family felt they were being let down because Kieran could not handle himself in the outside world. Even though they had some sympathy for Kieran they were disappointed with him and he never really received the nurturant acceptance and positive emotional feedback that is so essential for believing in himself. This cycle of rejection, lack of belief in himself, being ostracised by peers, and lack of inclusion, meant that Kieran never learned the skills of social intercourse because he never had any practice. He had never been part of the group of lads hanging around bantering, slagging or testing each other's mettle in the safety of belonging to the group. So when he was jeered, slagged or put down two things happened. Firstly, because he wasn't perceived as being a member of his peer group, the slagging was much more vicious and cynical and as a result was felt much more personally by him. Secondly, because he had no practice and because he knew it was serious slagging he was unable to take it. This was more an admission that he did not know how to deal with it. The more he 'could not take it' the more he was jeered and put down.

So the question had to be asked: Where did Kieran learn the 'inability to cope' that was such a big part of his psychological make-up?

The answer to this question came accidentally. As part of our work together, Kieran and I agreed that there would be feedback to his parents. This took place with Kieran and his parents, but without the other members of the family. During the initial session with the family it became clear that the dynamics of the family were mirrored in the behaviours of all participants of the session and Kieran became spatially isolated from and emotionally separated from his parents. There was a shared perception among all three that he was the 'problem'. The distancing that was evident in the therapy room was symbolic of what was happening in reality.

More importantly, the unconscious issues that emerged during the session were fear of having a say, the father's lack of confidence in, and even embarrassment at his son, the mother's defending of her son against the father, and the father's defending of himself against any suggestion of fault on his part. There was also a very clear fear of expressing criticism.

The most significant happening was when Kieran suggested that his mother should come to see me. It was from this point on that the issue of a 'circle of aggressive fear' was taken out of the unspoken, unsaid, unmentionable and unconscious part of the family's world.

The characteristic atmosphere of the family was one of domination, unquestioning control, collusion and defensive passivity. This was the surface atmosphere but it masked the repressed hurt and anger of not having a say, and not being listened to. All other members of the family were sucked into the characteristic atmosphere and therefore were at its mercy, and became not only part of it, but also agents of it, and victims of it.

The key issue in all of this belonged initially to Robert, the father, whose domineering demands for his own way were realised with the help of the fear and resultant collusion of the mother. For the sake of peace she would agree and go along with his unreasonable demands and his silencing and putting down of the children.

While it became clear early on that the key person was the father, there was a continued acting out of the family situation in the father's unconscious avoidance of his role in dealing with this. It was accepted only after many avenues had been tried.

Robert, the father, it turned out was actually ready to take on the task of breaking the circle of aggression, because he had realised that he, more than any of the others, had ownership of this issue. He also had reached a point in his personal growth where he wanted to address some important issues in his own life and he knew that these issues were affecting the other members of his family.

It became clear that the aspects of his son that he was ashamed of, and that he could not face, were in fact those issues in himself that he was embarrassed about. His deep personal hurt and shame at what he felt he had done to his family was a realisation that needed to be 'held' and nurtured carefully so that it did not become guilt. It was important for Robert to acknowledge and accept what was his to own, and to take it back. But it was just as important that he did not become taken over by blame and guilt as this could block his movement forward.

In accepting the negative aspects of his own make-up Robert will begin to develop an accepting and valuing attitude to his son.

Robert's willingness and courage in being the person to break the circle of aggression and abuse will provide the space for the mother to withdraw her collusion and to develop her own 'masculine principle' of positive personal power.

The main point to be taken from this case is the way in which the unconscious issues of one powerful person within the group, if not dealt with, can become the issues of any or all members of the family.

What we see here is a situation where the normal healthy masculine energy of the father has become brutalised by his lack of belief in himself, and has sucked out the well of creative and positive energy of those over whom he has authority. The loss of this positive spirit leaves the person/child unable to develop the abilities needed for emotional self-care and survival at home or out in the world. The ego strength to survive in a social grouping or the necessary balance of assertiveness and acceptance to engage in a relationship on equal terms with another person, cannot develop without this positive creative energy.

This case helps us to see the dangers of creating a 'bulliable personality' where the person has his creative survival energy stifled by the negative father complex of the domineering father. This is not the only characteristic atmosphere where the 'bulliable personality' is created but it helps us to understand some of the possible reasons why some people seem to be more easily bullied than others.

7

INCLUSION AND EXCLUSION

.﹏

The feeling of belonging provides the person with one of the most important bases for mental well-being. As a child the need to belong is expressed in many ways and the belonging need is dependent on others in the child's life for fulfilment. Within the family the child's belonging need is dependent mainly on the ability of the parents to include the child in family life.

Satisfying the belonging need in children is fundamental to their self-esteem, their feeling of worth, and their feeling of being safe.

From birth children need to feel that they are part of some-thing bigger and stronger than themselves, that they can be looked after and minded. Though they may often rebel against this caring and try to break away from it, especially during the adolescent years, it is essential for them to feel a strong connection to the family in which they live. The strength of this bond and the dependability of it are what reassures children. Ironically, and what is sometimes difficult for the parents to accept, is the fact that the better the sense of belonging for children as they grow in a family the more able they are to leave the family.

As adults the belonging need is just as strong and just as much in need of expression. Whether it is in the workplace, in the family, or at play, the need to belong to a group, where individu-als are made to feel that they are a part of the group, gives a feeling of warmth and security which is essential to their overall psycho-logical well-being. Whatever group people belong to, they need to feel that it is able to meet their needs as individuals and as a part of the group.

In exercising and satisfying the need to belong there are two important dynamics at work among the individuals themselves and among the group to which they want to belong.

Being accepted in a group either at work or at home involves accommodation to the needs of the group, and it also requires assertiveness and a willingness to fight our way in. Success within the group demands the ability and confidence to promote ourselves, and a belief that we are good enough to be a part of the group. It involves feeling that the group needs us in it, but that we will not change too much or completely surrender our individuality for the good of the group. Being wanted by the group should mean being wanted for ourselves, as we are, and if a group demands excessive change from us in order to be accepted, then that group is wrong for us and should be avoided.

Having a scapegoat in a group is an example of a situation where an individual is rejected by the group, and the negative side of the group is projected on to this member. Fear of being scapegoated puts pressure on individuals to change so that they will be accepted. The underlying difficulty here is that if people change solely to be accepted by the group, they are living out the group's expectations. They are not being accepted for who they are and are therefore not really a part of the group. They cannot experience the deep warmth of being enclosed in the security of the group. This is the feeling of being needed, being wanted, and being of some value to the group.

An important aspect of belonging to a group is seen where people wish to be part of a group but the group isolates and excludes them. This is often seen at its most natural in the playground where the child complains: 'They won't let me play with them.' It is also a feature in family situations where a member has been excluded because of his or her behaviour.

Belonging is a two-way process in that being part of a group or family depends on the group and on the person. For children, belonging is more about the willingness of the group to accept them, than it is about their own openness to belong. For adults, being open to the possibility of belonging makes it easier for us to be taken in to the group. Our own personal history of belonging, particularly in relation to our family, has a significant effect on how well we are able to belong. If we have grown up in a situation where we have been rejected by our family, or where we have been excluded, we will find that we have not developed the skills that enable us to belong. The experience of exclusion, of not feeling that we belong, undermines our sense of self-worth, engenders mistrust and resentment towards the group, and so makes it difficult to belong. Where people have grown up in a situation of not belonging to their family, they are not familiar with the positive, warm feelings that accompany belonging and will find it difficult to become part of a group as they will be uncomfortable with these feelings.

➤ As we have said it is important to be open to the possibility of belonging and much of this is shaped by our past history of belonging. Being open to belonging means giving the group the benefit of the doubt and having a positive attitude. The model of belonging that we carry in the accumulated well of our experience and being, enhances or damages our capacity to gain entry to groups.

➤ Belonging is also helped by being assertive and expressive of who we are. This honesty about who we are makes the group more willing to accept and take us in. It means that when we are accepted within the group we know we are there because of who we are in our own right rather than on the basis of meeting group criteria.

➤ Hand in hand with this is the acceptance by us as individuals of the group needs and our willingness to fit in with the norms of the group without losing our individuality.

➤ In developing our ability to belong we need to

- be willing to contribute
- allow ourselves to be influenced by others
- accept that we will have to concede some of our autonomy
- present the real self to the group.

When people want to gain entry to a group that does not want them there are a number of dynamics at work. Firstly, the individuals feel left out and isolated. In addition they feel the resistance of the group which is not so much resisting their entry as protecting its own integrity.

The group already has its own integrity, is a complete group and will resist attempts to breach that integrity. If the needs of the group are met by including a new member then a space will be made but where the group does not want an intruder it will resist. We see this phenomenon in many areas of life. When refugees arrive in another country there is both conscious and unconscious resistance to what is seen as intruders. The perception that they are a threat to the emotional, social and political status quo generates a strong resistance to their inclusion.

The underlying feelings of fear that our way of living will be damaged, that the intruders will threaten our society, kindle the unconsciously transmitted fear of invasion that is part of the collective unconscious. Including others in our world requires us to be confident about who we are and to be able to hold on to our way of life without fearing that it will be diminished. We need to have confidence that our world is strong enough to assimilate newness. In short we need to be comfortable with change.

In the workplace fears of survival and self-preservation are stronger and ambition and power complicate the issue further. Joining a new place of work is most often a response to a perceived need and it may not be welcomed by the existing members of staff, who may perceive the new arrival as a threat to the social and economic hierarchy of the group.

The process of initiation into the group involves change for both the individual and the group in as much as the individual will have to be seen to take on the norms, attitudes and values of the group before being included as an accepted member of the group. In extreme cases this can mean that the person has to submit totally to the demands of the group. Where this happens it causes the group to become dysfunctional.

The group itself is changed not only in terms of size and configuration, but more importantly in terms of the relationships of the people within the group. The introduction of a new member to the group changes the balance within the group, changes the personal preferences of the individual members of the group and upsets the emotional status quo. This is very well illustrated when a baby is born. Where the child is the first-born in a family it changes the relationship of the parents to each other. Up to this point they could devote their time to each other, the only emotional demands came from each other, and all their communication was directly between the two of them. When another person becomes a part of the existing group the whole dynamic changes. There is now a third person in the group so it is bigger. Although in most cases the new group member is wanted and cherished and the 'group' is happy to include the new member, some of the changes are difficult to cope with. Where previously communication was direct now some messages are sent through the child though this is mainly an unconscious transference of both feeling and information. The attention which each of the parents was devoting to the other is now shared and lessened.

IMELDA'S STORY

Imelda is a woman in her fifties who now has chosen to live alone. She came to see me because she was feeling depressed, unable to cope with being isolated from her family and at the same time feeling that she had to be available for everybody who needed something done.

Imelda is one of a large family of boys and girls and she grew up in the rural Ireland of the 1950s. From her earliest memories she felt that her mother did not want her. Her mother continually physically beat her and reminded her that it would have been better if she had never been born. At a very early age Imelda had an accident, the scars of which are visible to this day. The feeling of being rejected by her mother was ever-present and in time became transmitted to other members of the family so that she felt that she was never accepted by them either. As a result she felt excluded, isolated and rejected during her time at home.

When I met with Imelda, her anger was overwhelming her. It was particularly directed at her mother. She was uncomfortable with the idea that she was angry about the things that had been done to her, and she found it difficult to accept that anyone should be angry with a parent. The fact that she was so nurturant to her own children was at once connected to her own experience as a child and at the same time it made it more difficult for her to accept what her mother had done to her. A number of times during our work together Imelda said she hated her mother, particularly because she felt that her mother was continually putting down her (Imelda's) children. Her anger had festered for so long that it had turned into revenge, an unwillingness to concede defeat and a desire to get back at her mother and members of her family.

Imelda had turned all her creative and nurturant energies into looking after her own children and one or two people outside her immediate family, and this was starting to create other difficulties. It was as if she was determined to prove her mother wrong and that part of her revenge was in giving her own children everything she had emotionally. She became over-protective of her children, and was unable to cope when anyone said anything negative about them. Her over-nurturing meant that her children felt they owned her and could have total control over her life. Even her grandchild was able to control her.

Imelda's inability to accept her anger as genuine meant that she turned it in on herself, and this was further complicated by her sense of frustration at not having her own emotional space. Finally she had very little say in her life and although in many ways she felt that she was looking after those who were important to her, she was angry, lonely, and missing her mother. Because there was no place for herself in her world, she was depressed.

The beginning of our work together was to legitimise her anger and to get it out from inside. She needed to accept that it was real and that it was justified. By allowing her to express it openly and without judgement she began to believe in herself. As long as it was turned in, it was negative and destructive and would continue to fester. It was also important to separate what her mother 'did to her', from her mother as a person. It was her mother who did these things but her mother was not the things. This was difficult as Imelda at this time wanted a focus for her anger, and her hatred and resentment towards her mother was so great, and she had harboured it for so long, that she thought nobody else had a right to intrude. However, she willingly accepted that she did not have the right to change her mother but that, by looking at her own issues, she could change her reaction to what had happened. This had the extra attraction that it was adding to the process of putting herself back into her life. As part of the process of changing her own world she began to set up healthy, strong boundaries to enable her to have a safe, personal space in her life. This necessitated asserting herself both with her own children and with other people who were her friends. There was still some abusive behaviour from some members of her family and this required Imelda to agree to take on skills to protect herself and to save herself. She learned how to verbally stand up to people, to use strong language if it was called for, and not to be put down.

One day she came in and said she was going on holiday on her own. She was on her way.

8

BOUNDARY
AND SPACE

One of the most difficult life situations that we need to nego-tiate is the dichotomy of boundary and space. To be emotionally and socially healthy each of us needs to have secure and strong boundaries around us and at the same time to have a safe, secure, individual space in which to be ourselves. The diffi-culty lies in the fact that the two concepts seem to be mutually exclusive and yet they are mutually dependent.

The secure, safe boundary that the child experiences in the womb becomes the aspiration for all relationships in the personal life both as a child and as an adult. It is an important emotional and psychological protection and is essential for us as individuals to feel secure and safe in life. The boundary is provided by fami-lies, schools, communities and all groups to which the person belongs, and is experienced in the form of feelings of belonging, feelings of being wanted and awareness that the other people in the group care about us, and care for us. The boundary provides a safe space in which we can not only survive but flourish. It is a supportive, nurturant, and protective emotional ring-fence that does not judge or condemn and is available to us in an unques-tioning way whenever it is needed.

At birth we need to be accepted within this boundary and to be held there, particularly during the early years. Where the boundary does not exist, is damaged or is undependable, we do not learn to trust those around us. A damaged or unsafe boundary occurs where the family is violent, where the parents are absent or where the child feels abandoned. Where a child is enclosed in an unsafe or abusive boundary, the ability to trust is damaged, the ability to belong is damaged, and the sense of individual and collective worth is damaged. These social and emotional inadequacies continue into adulthood where the need to be included, to belong and to be protected is part of the emotional make-up of all adults. Problems arise in a number of ways. Often the male adult is unable or unwilling to allow himself to be held within the boundary because he feels that it is an acknowledgement of failure or weakness. It can also happen that adults are not allowed within the boundary because they have been rejected by the group, the family or the workplace. But it is no less important for the well-being and mental health of the adult to feel safe and secure, and to feel a sense of belonging, surrounded by the strong emotional boundary of family, friends and colleagues.

At the same time the person needs to be allowed the space to grow, to extend emotionally and to be intact within the boundary. Emotional space is necessary so that the individuality of the person, and the integrity of the person, as a person separate from the group in which he or she lives, works or plays, is maintained. One of the most difficult aspects of life is to be able to live as a full individual while at the same time being a full member of the group. There are conflicting psychological forces at work as the individual and the group each try to maintain their own emotional and personal integrity. Each needs the other to survive but if either the individual or the group is allowed free rein it will take over. Therefore both the individual and the group need to be assertive of their own right to space and boundary, while at the same time being aware of the space and boundary needs of the other.

It is this constant interplay between individual needs, collective needs and the struggle for dominance and equilibrium that contains both the risk and the opportunity for the individual and collective society. Neither can have all the space it wants and neither can allow the other to have all the space it wants. The psychological well-being of both the community and the individual depends on this creative tension. If the conflict ceases it means that one of the sides is dominant and therefore that the other is acquiescent and so not healthy. A healthy society has a continuous seeking and maintaining of personal and collective space, a continuous setting up and shifting of boundaries, with the integrity of both the boundary and the space being mutually coexistent. This holds for children in their dealings with the family, the school, and the society in which they live. If there is an unhealthy boundary encompassing a closed, unquestioning, authoritarian approach to family life, to life in the classroom, or to the child's recreational activities, the child will suffer and become passive, unquestioning and resentful. The resentment will later manifest itself as anger and revenge at the realisation of not being able to cope with the psychological, social and emotional demands of the world. Where the boundary is damaged through violence, abandonment or broken trust, the emotional space of the individual is contaminated by fear and mistrust.

Within the boundary of the workplace, marriage or any other relationship, this creative tension allows each person to fight legitimately for his or her own space and to feel the satisfaction of having achieved this space. Where the personal boundary of the individual is damaged by the boundary of the group, and the needs of the individual are subsumed by the needs of the group, the person will lose any sense of separateness, individuality, or personal achievement. Whatever role he or she plays in the family or group will be seen more in the context of the group needs than the individual needs.

It is the personal space which allows the person to assert the right to be a man or woman, to be that person and to pursue the goal of individuality. The strong basic need for protection and safety is balanced against the strong need to be separate. Each is equally important and when the balance is right there is flux, movement of emotional energy and continuous challenge to the *status quo*.

It is only when the personal emotional space is contained within a secure and sensitive boundary which responds to the demands of the person within, that the balance between protection and growth is maintained.

Gardiner's work on multiple intelligences introduces the notion of spatial intelligence and spatial awareness. Spatial awareness refers to our ability to see ourselves as separate entities, both physically and psychologically, in the context of the people around us. It means being able to allow others to have a space in which to live, a space in which to grow. Intrinsic to this idea is the notion that in allowing others to have space we feel comfortable in our own space and do not feel the need to invade the space of others. One of the underlying causes of violence and aggression in society is the inability to respect the space of others. Invading the space of another person usually comes from being unhappy in one's own space, feeling that one's space is not as good as the other person's space. Arising from that feeling is the feeling that one is diminished simply through the existence of the other's space. Hence the perceived need to take it over.

Space is essential within a marriage where two people live so closely together, emotionally and physically, for much of their daily lives, and it is essential that both partners are allowed to have their own space in terms of time, feelings, and social activity. Having this space is not only good for the individuals but it will also enhance the partnership and make each of the partners more attractive to the other. The partnership or the relationship of marriage provides the boundary for the individuals within it. The ability of the partners to be flexible and sensitive to the space needs of the other, while at the same time maintaining the secure boundary within which each can survive, is essential to the health of the marriage.

Another aspect of having space concerns that allowed to children in a family. Children's right to their personal space is often overwhelmed by the family's desire to have strong, safe boundaries. Because children are not in a position to fight their corner within the family system, their space within the boundary of the family may be denied and this has ramifications for their lives as children and their later lives as adults. It is in the family that children mainly learn the model of boundary and space that they will take with them into adulthood.

The need for space and healthy boundaries is also part of the healthy workplace environment. Allowing individuals within the workforce to have their own working space, their own social space, and their own intellectual space is essential for the health and satisfaction of the individual and the group. This psychological space is symbolised by the physical work space designated to the person, by the way in which individuals are consulted about decision-making in the workplace, and in particular the way in which individual needs are considered. The maintaining of a strong, flexible boundary is seen in the way in which the members of the workplace are loyal, share collective responsibility, share their triumphs and their failures and are included in the decision-making.

RACHEL'S STORY

Rachel is the youngest of a large family of high achievers. Her parents are both strong, caring people who want the best for all their children. Both parents are self-reliant and independent people who believe that they know what is best for their children.

Rachel is a bright, talented and sensitive young woman who has ambitions to go to college. In primary school she was the model child who never did anything wrong, always followed the rules and pleased her parents and teachers completely. Her parents naturally were extremely proud of her and did everything for her. This meant that Rachel never had to fight her corner. She never made mistakes and therefore never learned to cope with the idea of failure. She was never challenged and of course, because her own needs coincided with those of her parents, she always got what she wanted. All through primary school her behaviour and her achievements matched the expectations of her parents and both Rachel and her parents gradually and unconsciously became idealising partners.

I first met Rachel as a Leaving Certificate student, talented, intelligent, capable, and popular with her peers. All her siblings had been successful and naturally there were expectations that she would also do well. Her parents came to me because they were concerned that she was moody, withdrawn and conflictual, and they were worried that she might damage herself.

Rachel presented as bright and caring, quiet and unafraid. It was noticeable that she was much more reticent when her parents were present. At family sessions there was a very strong enveloping of Rachel, in particular by her father, but supported by the mother. Rachel was referred to as 'pet' and the phrase 'we only want the best for you' was used continually.

Rachel defended herself by turning her face away, crying and retreating into herself. The family were acting out, in the session, the behaviours that were typical of their life at home and that had led to the difficulties. On her own Rachel became open, jovial, talkative and assertive while in her parents' presence it was the opposite.

At home Rachel had become difficult, oppositional and secretive. She appeared to be deliberately going against her parents' wishes and the main way in which she showed her disregard for her parents' wishes was by spending long periods on the family 'phone.

At school her performance deteriorated and she began to lose interest in her work and in school generally. What the parents had done with the other children in their family had been successful and they saw no reason why it should not be the same for Rachel. The more they tried to intervene and to supervise, the more distant and oppositional Rachel became. The surface issues were opposition, being difficult and non-cooperation on Rachel's part, and protecting, caring and trying to help, on the parents' part. The underlying issues were much different.

On her own in the therapy room Rachel began to describe her feelings of being restricted both personally and socially, of being over-cosseted and of being spancelled in such a way that she felt she was not free to do anything without her parents knowing about it and consenting. She resented this and saw it not just as a lack of say in her own life, but also as her parents showing no confidence in her. Her reaction and indeed her only choice was to take them on. She was not yet able to confront them in an open and positive way. Her parents took her opposition as disrespect, ingratitude and not in her own best interest. In addition unconsciously the parents were unhappy about their youngest daughter's moves to emotional and personal independence because, since Rachel was the 'last' of their children, they would then feel in some way unneeded when she was gone. Rachel's unexpressed reasons for her behaviour were her need to be independent, to make decisions and to choose her own friends.

Her parents' story was that Rachel was unhappy in her previous school and had asked to move to another, where she became even more unhappy. Underlying the change of schools was the parents' anxiety about the friends she had in her first school. Rachel's story was that it was very much her parents who had wished her to move, although she did not agree with it. While there was some truth in both their stories, i.e. some common reality, there were also a lot of areas where the parents' reality differed greatly from Rachel's reality. And there were a lot of unconscious issues which neither Rachel nor her parents had considered.

Rachel's behaviour was a direct protest, a way of saying to anyone who would listen: I'm old enough and grown-up enough and mature enough to run my own life. Let me out of this emotional strait-jacket and give me my own space to show you, and to prove to me, that I can do this. Her protest was to exaggerate the 'phone contact with her friends as a way of getting at her parents and as a way of satisfying her need for revenge. There were also outbursts of anger and resentful silences which were Rachel's way of avoiding talking to her parents, and of getting at them. Naturally her parents became angry and even more restrictive.

We approached this from the perspective of each person in the group becoming aware of his or her own issues, reasons and needs, while at the same time trying to allow some of the other's reality to overlap into their consciousness. We looked at being aware of the needs of the group and how each person has a need for space within the boundary of the group. Allowing Rachel the space and support to do things that they did not necessarily agree with, while at the same time maintaining a strong family support and boundary, were essential for Rachel to flex her growing adult feelings. At the same time this freeing of their daughter to be herself was taking away much of the unnecessary worry that her parents had. So they were creating more space for themselves. For Rachel, becoming aware of her underlying need for independence and her resentment at having this denied, was a help to her in acknowledging her parents' right to the same space and the boundary of her love.

9

PARENTING

The problem with parenting is that we can never get it right. The good thing would be if we could accept the limitations of our position and our performance as parents. The best we can hope for is to be good enough parents. However hard we try, we make mistakes, make wrong decisions, hurt our children's feelings and punish them. But still it works out in the end. Our children grow up, become adults, and live their lives for the most part as effective adults.

When children are born they come into a world that is already in existence, that has its own way of doing things and into which the children have to fit whether they like it or not.

Parenting is about achieving a balance between what is best for children and what is best for parents, with neither parents nor children getting too much or too little. Difficulties arise when this balance is not maintained and either parents invest too much of themselves in children, or children are neglected or abandoned emotionally by parents who insist on investing all their energy in meeting their own selfish needs.

In the first situation, where parents invest too much in their children, idealisation occurs. Idealisation arises from the natural and necessary need of parents to provide for their children, not only for the children's sake, but to satisfy their own strong emotional need to protect and guarantee their own future. It is the parents' unconscious satisfaction of the need to survive not just for the duration of their actual lives, but to continue their existence through their children after their death. This instinct for survival is what helps parents to look after children and helps

to guarantee the healthy survival of children. Providing for
children, nurturing, protecting and caring for them is in reality a
form of self-preservation. Where the instinct remains unconscious
and is not acknowledged, the natural predisposition of parents to
protect and to nurture is funnelled into a powerful drive to ensure
their own survival, which extinguishes the desire to meet the
needs of the children, and manifests itself in the behaviour of
parents as over-protection, inflation of the children's worth and
over-expectation of success for them. Where idealisation occurs
parents are so close to their children that there is an emotional
and personal fusion of identities similar to what happens in the
womb. This means that in everyday situations children do what
the parents want, because they feel that this is necessary for them
to survive and because they feel that this is really what themselves want. Parents follow a similar path, trying to realise their
own ambitions, and live out the unlived aspects of their lives
through their children. This results in frustration for parents and
children.

Where there is neglect or abandonment by parents, it is not
only the children who suffer. A particular situation which occurs
in modern society is that of the parent who is absent because of
work demands. This phenomenon was in the past more likely to
be characterised by an absent father but it is now the norm for
both parents to work outside the home. Very often the focus tends
to be on the possible damage to the children through such
parental absenteeism, but there is also damage to the parent. Apart
from the effects on the relationship between parents and children
there is the unacknowledged gap in the emotional life of the
parents. In the case of the father this is a lessening of the caring,
nurturing, feeling side which is so much a part of the emotional
balance between masculine and feminine qualities, required for a
psychologically healthy life. In the case of the mother, being absent
for excessive periods creates a similar lacuna in her emotional
world, an inability to honour her mothering, nurturing, caring
role, which leaves a deficit in the overall emotional package of her

person. This lessening of the mothering role for a woman has implications for her as a person and as a woman.

MASCULINITY AND FEMININITY

The role required in the workplace for both men and women makes demands that are more in the masculine realm of hunter, gatherer, provider and less in the feminine realm of carer and nurturer. Hence there is a risk that the fundamental femininity of the person can be threatened as more and more of the masculine traits are taken on, to satisfy the demands of the workplace.

There are different implications for parents where the balance of the masculine and feminine in the parenting equation is skewed to either the masculine or the feminine. Both men and women have potential for masculine and feminine within them. The masculine principle or *animus* is more at home in the male and is seen in such traits as individualistic pushing out, a willingness to confront and the need to take risks; it can be summed up as a harder, more judging approach to life, with a sense of directness and immediate gratification about it. The feminine principle or *anima* is more at home in the female and shows itself as a greater desire for relationship and connection, has more of a soft feel to it, and is characterised by a greater desire for gathering in, reconciliation and tolerance of difference.

Both men and women have the capacity for masculinity and femininity, and there is a need for a balance between *anima* and *animus* within each of us. One of the most important issues today is the need to honour both masculine and feminine principles. This is a requirement within each of us individually, within each relationship, and within society as a whole. Honouring the masculine is not tantamount to extinguishing the feminine and the aim is to achieve a balance of masculine and feminine principles within each person, a balance that reflects the needs of being a man or a woman. For the man it is necessary to honour his masculine side, to give value to his need to push out, his need to compete, and his need to master his environment. Honouring his masculinity is essential for his perception of himself as a man, and to provide a strong base from which to express his feminine side. If his *animus* is too weak, is not valued or is hidden, his masculinity will be extinguished. It is only within the setting of a strong, open and proud masculine principle that a man can be unafraid of his *anima*.

Protecting the *anima* in women has become an issue with the changes in lifestyles, in particular as more women work outside the home. The workplace exercises aspects of the person that are more in the masculine realm. Having to compete in the workplace, taking risks, operating more in the logical side of the brain, all make it difficult to honour the feminine. If the *anima* is set aside, is not valued or is denied, the caring, nurturing, tolerant aspects of the female psyche become diminished. It is only out of a healthy, affirmed and acknowledged feminine principle that the woman can healthily connect into her *animus*.

An over-developed *animus* in a woman turns her into a domineering, inflexible and controlling mother who is unable to tap into her soft *eros*. An over-developed *anima* in a man turns him into a weak, indecisive and easily controlled individual who has lost contact with his masculine principle.

LONE PARENTING

In the case of the one-parent family the provision of a healthy masculine-feminine mix for the child is in some ways easier. Where the parenting is in the hands of either the father or mother it is usual for the parent to attempt to compensate for the absent parent. Initially this can cause the caring parent some guilt and anxiety as he considers whether he is able to satisfy the father and mother needs. This leads to a greater effort and therefore greater consciousness and can mean that the child in the lone-parent family has a more stable model of the masculine/feminine mix. What is important here is the fact that both men and women have the capacity to meet feminine and masculine needs in a child. Having both parents present and attentive in the child's life is the ideal situation as it allows the child to have immediate access to masculine and feminine modelling, but where the child lives with one parent both the masculine and feminine principles are present. A young child will not be conscious of acquiring masculine or feminine traits, and will for the most part assimilate what is transmitted to him or her.

In both two-parent and lone-parent situations the requirement is for the parents to bring to conscious awareness their masculine and feminine 'sides' and to ensure that the child experiences both. It is common for difficulties to arise where two parents have separated and one has custody but both are caring for the child. If the separation issues of the parents have not been addressed and dealt with, the unconscious residue of the negative aspects of the separation will be transmitted to the child. This is especially so if one or other parent feels that the other has 'got a better deal' from the courts and that one or other is not being allowed enough time with the child. Each parent may be so taken up with issues of resentment, revenge and unhappiness that the caring feminine principle is annihilated by the exaggerated masculine side. It is helpful in such situations for both parents as far as possible to have flexible and satisfying time with their child.

GRANDPARENTING

Grandparenting brings its own set of interesting challenges, complicated by the feel-good factor that continually surrounds the image of grandparent and the desire of the grandparents themselves to be benign parents who can be seen by the child as a refuge from the reality of parents. Yet grandparenting presents a unique opportunity to contribute to the growth of the child and the family as a unit.

It is often seen as second-chance parenting: a chance to make up for the mistakes made first time around and also a chance for the grandparents to parent the parents. It can be difficult for parents who become grandparents to differentiate between parenting and grandparenting. And of course it is a chance for the grandparents to show off their parenting skills to their children, i.e. the parents of the young child. Achieving the balance between being helpful and being intrusive and critical is the difficult and important bit.

One of the changes which modern work practices and life-styles have brought is the lessening of the role of the extended family. In traditional non-western societies the welfare of the child is shared among all members of the extended family and a more over-arching and therefore effective set of emotional and behavioural checks and balances is built into the system. There is evidence that the influence of the extended family or at least that of the grandparents is being reasserted as many young parents now experience both the economic and personal need to work outside the home. Grandparenting presents many opportunities and chal-lenges for the child's parents and grandparents. For children it is an opening up of a wider world outside the narrow focus of their own immediate world of reality and it reassures them that there is security and continuity in their world as they see that their parents have somebody to look after them. The dangers of grand-parenting arise in two ways. Firstly, it is essential that children see and experience their grandparents and learn about a different world, but if the grandparents have unresolved, unconscious issues around their own parenting they may seek to deal with these through over-doing the grandparenting. They may unconsciously take over the role of parent and displace the real parents. Secondly, they may want to ensure that their children do a better job than they themselves did and try to take over the parenting. Both these possibilities show up as grandparents being too intrusive and interfering in the work of parents, and while the motive may be 'for your own good', the result is that the real parents feel crit-icised, inadequate and undermined.

CHALLENGES FOR PARENTS

➤ Because of the nature and closeness of the parent-child relationship it is easy to become too close to the child and in so doing to stifle difference and individuality. It is important to treat our children as separate, different and unique individuals. We must try to remember that our children are not us, that they have a separate being and different needs, and possess their own innate skills to deal with their environment. By being conscious of our own individuality and by being aware of the separateness of each child, we will be able to withdraw any negative projections which we have put on to the child and therefore free ourselves as well as the child.

➤ In this way parents can learn to value their own separateness and individuality, and this frees them to have a life of their own. It is a much healthier model of relationship to show to a child, where the adult is able to have a life that is separate from the person with whom he or she is in a relationship while not in any way diminishing the relationship. The child can see that it is possible to be in a relationship with either a peer or an adult and at the same time be free to have other relationships. The benefits for the parents are obvious.

➤ If we identify too much with the role of parent it will be difficult for us to be ordinary people with our children. They need to see us as parents, and to know that there is a big person there who can take care of them. But they also need to have the experience of relating to their parent as just another person and so the parent needs to relate to the child as a person. If parents can see themselves as people who also happen to be parents, partners, tennis players etc, they will be able to be people in their own right and not be totally taken up with the parent identity. Being able to discard the persona of the parent, occasionally, allows the child to relate to the parent on an equal level.

➤ Because we want to provide for our children as best we can, and because we want our children to a have a better life than we had, we can easily fall into the perfect parent trap where we want everything to be perfect and where we are overly critical of our performance as parents. It is more helpful to our own development as people, to the health of the child, and to the development of the child as a future adult, as well as being much more in tune with the reality of our flawed world, if we adopt a position of being good enough parents. It allows us the freedom to be both real and flawed in the eyes of our children.

➤ The responsibility of the parent and the natural instinct of the parent is to be there for the child and to do what is necessary to bring the child to responsible and effective adulthood. In carrying out this function parents can sometimes do too much for their child.

For children, the effects of having too much done for them are:

- inability to cope on their own
- over-dependence on adults
- lack of belief in their own capabilities
- inability to make decisions.

For parents the effects of doing too much for children are:

- never seeing the children at their best
- never getting a real sense of pride from children's achievements, as it is never the children's own achievement
- fear of letting the children out on their own
- constant worry about children's welfare
- not having a life of their own because they are always more concerned about what the children are doing than what they themselves are about to do
- deep, hidden feelings of dissatisfaction with their own performance. They feel their children are not capable of acting independently and therefore intrude into their lives continually. This comes from parents' own self-doubt and the belief that they have not done well as parents.

The balance here is to be found in parents being conscious of their own lives, their own achievements and their children's capabilities. To be able to allow children to make mistakes, to fail, to take a risk and embarrass us in public, is very difficult but very necessary. An extremely important issue in the parenting process is that although the ultimate goal of childrearing is to enable children to become effective adults, it is essential that the immediate object of childhood is being a child. For both parent and child it is better that the child is seen as a child, not as a future adult.

CHALLENGES FOR GRANDPARENTS

➤ The most potent temptation for grandparents is to want to parent the parents. This arises through an unexpressed lack of confidence in their own record as parents. All parents have the potential to be good enough parents and for the most part uninvited and inappropriate intervention into the childrearing equation of another generation causes anger and feelings of inadequacy. It can have the effect of making the actual parents feel resentful at the intrusion of 'outsiders'. It also causes parents to feel inadequate in their parenting. It is more helpful to allow parents to make their own mistakes and for grandparents to be there in a supporting role.

➤ It is also likely that grandparents may try to compensate for the inadequacies of their own parenting by over-parenting their grandchildren. This is most likely to happen where the flaws in their own performance as parents are not acknowledged and remain unconscious, but surface unwittingly through their over-zealous attempts to be nice to their grandchildren. For grandparents it is useful to reflect on their own performance and to be unafraid to admit that they made some mistakes.

➤ As outside observers of the behaviour of the children and their parents and as perhaps silent commentators on the performance of the parents, it is inevitable that grandparents will see behaviours, approaches and attitudes that are different from the way they did it and that they may think are damaging to the children. The temptation is then strong to make up for what they see as parenting deficits, by lavishing affection, approval or material rewards on the children. It is much more helpful to let the parents parent and when the opportunity arises to offer guidance.

➤ The best role for grandparents might be to be there in a supporting role, a facilitating role for the parents in their work of parenting, and to act as an outer ring in a ring-fort of trust, safety and love, a ring-fort that is comprised of the various layers of family members. They are a significant part of the healthy family boundary, and this means being able to live with approaches they might not approve of.

➤ An important function of grandparents is to provide children with a stable point of reference in the children's world of time, space, attachment and separation. Grandparents represent, for children, evidence that there is continuity in life and that there is a future. The children are exposed to the task of dealing with the separation anxiety associated with departure, and death, in a way that is not immediate.

➤ The presence of grandparents reassures the children that their parents are not on their own, and that there are people there to care for their parents.

CHALLENGES FOR LONE PARENTS

For lone parents the challenge is the same as for two parents, with some additions. Lone parents have had to take on society's view that lone parenting is somehow not as effective as pair parenting. Where there are two parents who work together, who are conscious of themselves as people, where the masculine/feminine balance is good, it is clear that at a practical level it is easier to meet the needs of children. However, the lone parent has the same challenge of parenting, the same choice in regard to the level of parent-child relationship, and the same commitment to make.

➤ Being the only parent in the child's life has the advantage that there will be no ambivalence in terms of parenting approaches.

➤ The natural healthy dependence that parents and children share within the family boundary can sometimes become over-dependence. In a lone-parent family because there is usually one adult to service the emotional needs of all the children the emotional burden on the parent can mean that the parent's own emotional needs are neglected. In a similar way the parent may try to satisfy his or her own needs by depending too much on the child.

➤ It is important for lone parents to be secure and happy about their parenting skills. Because the lone-parent family system is still not fully accepted by society, lone parents may feel under more scrutiny and more uncertain of the acceptability of their parenting strategies. It is important for lone parents to acknowledge that their intuitive, inner, inherited skills are adequate for the purpose of meeting the needs of their children; skills such as believing in their own innate ability, not being afraid to ask for help, and being strong enough to ignore unwanted intervention in favour of their own judgement.

➤ For lone parents it is necessary to have lives of their own, separate from that of their family. Where they live their lives through the children they will not be able to develop themselves as people and will be too closely tied emotionally to their children.

➤ It helps a lot where lone parents are conscious of their own emotional, social and personal needs. If this awareness is present the children are not in danger of being the vehicle for meeting the adult's needs. Also it allows the parents to know their own needs and so gives them a better possibility of satisfying them.

➤ By dealing with their own attachment and separation issues, whether it is from parents or former partner, lone parents are in a better position to allow the children to separate, not to idealise, and not to become over-attached.

PETER'S STORY

Peter and Mary are the parents of a large family of boys. They live in a rural area and married when they were very young, having had little experience of other relationships.

Peter has a very strongly developed masculine principle and has an unfulfilled sense of adventure and risk which is a very active part of his unconscious being. He has very strong political beliefs and religious beliefs which are for the most part hidden.

Mary is a strong, controlling person with deeply held religious convictions, a strong *animus*, and a very deeply held belief in her own position in the family. Her family background is different from Peter's, in so far as her family owned land whereas Peter's family did not. Mary's inherited but unfulfilled ambition is projected into the lives of her children and they represent, for Mary in particular, the possibility of recovering the lost position and status of her family. There is an unconscious and unspoken belief that her family is superior to Peter's and this often comes out in the way she represents Peter to the children.

The story of Peter and Mary is one of dissatisfaction with their lives, a sense of the world being against them and of dreams that would never be fulfilled.

Mary, as a mother, invested all her emotional energy in her children, and always put herself second to their needs. As a result her relationship with Peter suffered and the children became more important than her husband in her life. But a more important issue was that she neglected her own emotional needs and developed a sense of self-devaluation that had its roots in her religion, her loss of status within her own family and the lack of power and say in her own life. This self-devaluation, though it had its roots in her own experiences, became a vehicle for expression in the lives of her children, where it was not only a spur for her ambition for them, but also an aspect of how she saw her children.

Peter had very little opportunity to develop his masculine need for adventure, control, and authority. His work was such that he had no say in that area of his life, and this denial of the masculine principle in the public part of his world caused him to exaggerate it in the home where he became authoritarian, aggressive and closed emotionally. The money he earned was controlled by Mary, which further denied the opportunity to validate his masculinity. The only aspect of his masculinity that was honoured was the providing instinct and the procreative instinct. His work meant that he spent very little time with his children and this, coupled with the fact that Mary was so close to them, meant that his position as authority figure, and his emotional bond with them, was mediated through the mother. This emasculation was further highlighted by the fact that if he needed money he had to ask for it both at work and at home.

The traditional perception that rearing the children was the responsibility of the mother was strengthened by the emotional and material circumstances of the family. Mary was very protective of her children in public but could never bring herself to praise or express pride in them in the intimacy of the family. She became more and more enveloped by the success or failure of her children with the result that her whole sense of worth was dependent on factors outside of herself. She had no identity of her own, and consequently no sense of personal value. If her children were doing well she felt good, if they were in trouble she felt bad.

Peter's way of survival was to identify with his work. When things went wrong he escaped into his work and because his work was so valuable and so necessary to the well-being of the family, this was an acceptable escape. It also meant that there was an emotional gap developing between him and his children and mostly the only physical contact with the children would be for disciplinary reasons. Given that Mary had such close contact with the children, had such a strong attachment to them, and that there was now a 'negative' attachment developing between the children and Peter, it often happened that the children would side with the mother against the father. As a result Peter became emotionally detached from his children.

In the middle of all this Peter and Mary had little or no life together. They had very little opportunity, or means, to socialise either individually or together and very little opportunity to talk. The unconscious resentments that they had towards each other, Mary's resentment towards Peter's lack of ambition, and Peter's resentment towards what he saw as Mary turning his children away from him, made it difficult to develop a close relationship. So both were unhappy with each other and with themselves.

Peter's anger at being deprived of his true masculine role in life was being expressed verbally and physically towards Mary and the children. He occasionally tried to escape through alcohol, but in fact he could never escape and he was unable to bring his unconscious shadow to consciousness. He reacted aggressively to any suggestion of weakness, negativity or anger and was unable to accept himself as he was. Mary buried her anger and disappointment in feelings of martyrdom and abandonment and was unable to accept her shadow or to acknowledge her own worth as a person.

Although she was closely attached to her children, and although she managed to maintain a strong emotional hold on them, Mary never achieved an emotional intimacy that would satisfy the feminine principle of deep friendship and love. Peter's emotional detachment was both cause and effect and because fear was a significant factor in the father-son relationship he was unable to get close to his children in a way that was fulfilling and unconditional.

_____

10

SEPARATION
AND
ATTACHMENT

⌣

From the moment of birth our lives are a series of attachments being made, attachments being broken, separations from loved ones, wanting attachments that we cannot have, wanting separations that we are unable to achieve. Attachment and separation are the basic emotional currency of our lives. All the separations we experience in our lives are emotional re-enactments of the trauma of birth infused with the fear of abandonment. The separation anxiety and grieving which is experienced in varying degrees by the child starting school, the adolescent going to college for the first time, the girlfriend/boyfriend breaking up, the partner separating after years of marriage, or the person grieving the death of a loved one, all have one thing in common: they unconsciously resonate with the emotional experience of separating from the womb.

When children are born they experience the most traumatic separation of their lives, where they are forcibly taken from a secure, nurturing and safe environment into a hostile, competitive and unfamiliar world. This of course is a necessary part of the life process, but the emotional stamp of birth remains part of people's overall emotional make-up and is so strongly imprinted that it is retrieved each time they experience separation during their lives. The fear of abandonment lies dormant in the unconscious of children and adults and is reactivated whenever separation becomes an issue. This fear of abandonment can be so strong in both children and adults that people may find it hard to achieve separation or to cope with the accompanying emotional distress which we call separation anxiety. The way in which the family deals with the occasions when separation anxiety comes up during childhood significantly shapes the level of fear of abandonment in the individual. It also shapes the capability of people to form attachments and to deal with separations in their lives. Separation may take place through the 'acceptable' procedures such as hospitalisation, starting school, adoption, or death. It may also occur through experiences that are not seen as acceptable such as emotional absence from children or actual physical abandonment of children. These unacceptable separations bring with them the added baggage of guilt and blame.

Attachment is a normal, healthy and necessary bond that exists in all people. It is a symbolic representation of the umbilical connection between mother and child while the child is in the womb. This physical connection is the lifeline of the child in the womb and its psychological equivalent is the feeling of closeness, connection and belonging that is experienced by two people who love each other.

Unhealthy attachment occurs where two people, mother/daughter, father/son, marriage partners are so close that their identities are fused and neither has room to be himself or herself. This type of relationship usually manifests itself as idealisation where each sees the other as being perfect and there is no room for any form of personal individuality.

Unhealthy separation occurs in childhood where parents are absent from children for prolonged, even permanent, periods of time without any attempts to support them or to be there when they need support, which, in reality is all of the time.

Residues of all the relationships that we have ever had will always remain in our unconscious psyche, and will form an important invisible emotional filter and reference point for forming future relationships. Healthy separation, being able to let go of a relationship when it is over, in the case of a healthy relationship, or when it is necessary as in the case of an abusive relationship, is an important aspect of healthy living. Letting go of a relationship, or allowing the other person to end a relationship, accepting that the relationship is finished, is related to the experiences we have had in letting go and being let go in all our former relationships and in particular it is heavily influenced by the way in which we experienced separation and attachment in the family situation. This is especially true of the primary separation and attachment experience between mother and child, and the way in which this primary experience mediates all other separation and attachment experiences.

In an abusive relationship a dependency can grow and the people in the relationship can each find it difficult to break out or to separate from each other. For those being abused there is the sense of being familiar with the abusive relationship and of this being the only environment in which they can cope. Added to this is the fear that if they leave familiar emotional and personal surroundings they will not be able to cope. In an abusive relationship the parties are not allowed to develop skills for survival, so the fear of not being able to survive on their own keeps them in the relationship and makes them dependent on those who are in fact damaging them.

This form of damaging dependency is possible in all relationships. In the mother-child relationship it may take the form of an idealising relationship where mothers put the children on a pedestal and invest all their hopes and expectations in them. The children never have to take emotional risks in their lives. In their mother's eyes they are perfect and they never learn the reality of surviving in the emotional marketplace which is the real world. Therefore their ability to acquire emotional survival skills is never allowed to develop. This form of abusive relationship is both difficult to identify and difficult to deal with because it masquerades as love and appears to be above criticism. The net result of such an abusive attachment is what is often termed the 'spoiled child', where everything is done because 'I love you and because I want the best for you and I don't want you to have to suffer the way I did when I was a child'. Any attempt to name this 'idealising dependency' will be genuinely resisted because it is for the most part an unconscious experience and is usually the result of the parents' genuine love for their children and their wish to provide for them in a way that both appeases their unease about their own childhood, and also their need to provide for their children.

ADULT SEPARATION

Similar difficulties present themselves in adult relationships where one or the other partner in the relationship wishes to end the relationship. Where a close, perhaps intimate relationship exists between two adults a strong attachment will form. Attachment is a healthy dependency where both parties benefit from the closeness, trust and sense of connectedness that form the basis for attachment. The longer the relationship has been in existence the stronger the attachment and the more difficult the separation. In the case of marriage break-up where the couple will have shared many close experiences such as having children, the separation is extremely difficult.

For both the person wanting separation and the person wishing to stay in the relationship the consequences of the separation can be:

- ➤ extreme sadness
- ➤ unexplained anger
- ➤ wanting to hurt the other partner
- ➤ feelings of jealousy
- ➤ desire for revenge
- ➤ fears of loneliness, and being alone
- ➤ fear of not being able to cope
- ➤ fear of being abandoned
- ➤ feelings of rejection and inadequacy
- ➤ feelings of suspicion.

These signs can manifest themselves during separation and the underlying fears are the same for both parties, the person who is 'causing' the separation and the person who may not want to separate. Separation causes anxiety in the main because it carries resonances of all the other separations we have experienced and in particular those that have been traumatic and perhaps abusive. It carries memories of the fears associated with other traumatic separations and these fears are present whether the person is active in the separation or not. In addition, in the case of marital separation there are feelings of having been wronged, and of wanting to get back at the other person. There is a natural feeling that 'my' situation is much worse than 'yours', and feelings of jealousy and anger if one feels that the other is receiving undeserved support.

NEGATIVE ATTACHMENT

In the case of an unhealthy attachment such as an abusive relationship between two adults, be they lovers, partners, spouses or friends, the difficulties are much the same with the added complication that there is a fear element. In the abusive relationship the attachment has been brutalised so that one person treats the other as an object rather than a person. This means that the relationship is not on equal terms. One person believes that he or she owns the other and has the right to control that person. There is the problem that the person being abused may become habituated in the role of victim and through fear of being unable to cope in an unfamiliar environment, may find it difficult to move away from the abusive attachment. In trying to separate from an abusive relationship the person who is suffering abuse may be so afraid of the abuser and so 'attached' to this person that he or she will exaggerate the attachment and closeness. Such an attachment to the abuser can on the surface appear to be a close relationship and can be extremely difficult to break out of.

More recently another dimension to the separation issue has come to prominence: the unwillingness of one partner to allow the other to separate. In such cases the relationship will have been an abusive one, and one partner, usually the man, treats his girlfriend, wife, partner, as an object which he thinks he owns and therefore controls. He may refuse to allow the other person to move out from the relationship. His own fear of abandonment, his fear that he won't be able to survive on his own, is preventing him from letting the other person go. The only way he can guarantee that he won't be abandoned is by controlling the woman, by threatening her and by forcible attachment. His fears of separation and abandonment are infantile and undeveloped, and coupled with a brutalised masculine principle he seeks to control and force the woman to stay with him. This is a case of negative and abusive attachment taking over the psyche of one person to the detriment of another.

Finding the balance between healthy attachment and the attachment which is too close and too strong can be very difficult for the person who has not experienced and coped with attachment and separation in a holding, supportive and caring way.

➤ Accept that it is okay to experience the need to attach to others who are close to us, and that when we separate, whether it is a minor separation or a major separation, we will experience doubt, uncertainty, fear of being alone and anxiety about surviving on our own.

➤ By being aware of the need in others to feel attached to us we are better able to accept our own attachments in our life, and to deal with the separation.

➤ Separation is a two-way process in that the 'active' person in the process, i.e. the person who is causing the separation (the mother of the child going to school, the girl or boy who wants to end a relationship, the partner who is seeking a divorce), will experience the anxiety and sadness of separation to the same extent as the other person who is 'passive' in the separation. Knowing and accepting this can be a help, particularly in the case of adults where each party to the separation may feel that the other has the easier time, and uses this 'handy excuse' to avoid moving on from sadness and grief.

➤ Separation is more manageable if both the active and the passive parties become aware of what is happening, try to be conscious of their own and the other's behaviour, and try to be active in what is happening in the separation.

➤ Separating from children starting school has similarities to all separation but also has distinct issues, mainly due to the fact that the children are too young to rationalise separation. Their experience of separation will be entirely at the emotional, instinctual and infantile level, and they will experience the fear but not be able to rationalise it. Usually they know they are going to school, and want to do this as a rite of passage, as an indicator to themselves and their peers and family that they are growing, but they will be unable to consciously deal with the separation and will not associate the physical symptoms they experience, with the separation from their parents. In addition the parents may not want to express the sadness they feel, perhaps in an unwise attempt to protect the children, and this presents a difficult task in particular for the parent who brings them to school.

➤ As we grow there are many issues, feelings and prejudices that are consigned to our unconscious and that have an effect on our behaviour. In relation to separation there are unconscious influences that can determine how successful we are at coping with separation anxiety. By becoming aware of our hidden issues, our unused and uncomfortable emotions, and events in our life that we usually avoid thinking about, we can take these issues out of the separation equation and see it for itself. This is particularly important when we are the 'active' party in the separation process.

➤ Separation anxiety is infused with the emotional memory of previous abandonments and fears of destruction, and it is by developing our own separate identity, our own separate life, our own separate living experience that we can acknowledge and live positively with our separation anxiety. Establishing our own ability to live separately and on our own is also essential

to our being able in adulthood to form healthy attachments.
➤ The separation-attachment dance is a lifelong process and the way in which we experienced this as children will have a crucial bearing on our later ability to form healthy attachments and be able to separate either from healthy relationships or from unhealthy relationships.

LAURA'S STORY

Laura was eight when I met her. The reason she came to see me was that her parents, more especially her mother, were concerned about her well-being, and in particular her behaviour. This is the story of how separation affects all those in the surrounding psychological area of the separation, and how those who are not actively involved in the separation process will also experience the effects of separation anxiety.

It is also the story of how the separation of parents, however necessary or good in its own right, sucks in the child who has no control over what is happening.

Laura's parents decided to live apart even though this was more her father's wish than her mother's. They were both experiencing the pain of separation even though it was different for each of them. The father wanted to separate while the mother did not, but accepted that it was necessary and was going to happen anyway.

For the mother the separation issues were feelings of insecurity, feelings of worthlessness at being rejected, anger at what her husband and his new partner were doing to her, and fear of isolation and aloneness. This fear of being alone, fear of not being able to cope, and fear for her own safety was the contaminating and linking factor in all the feelings that the mother was experiencing. The father was feeling resentful at what he felt was the mother's unwillingness to allow him to go. He was also feeling sadness at the end of the relationship, but was unable to express or acknowledge these feelings because he felt he did not have the right to do so.

Laura was experiencing separation in a more uncertain way in that she was not sure who she was going to be away from. She was also feeling sorry for her parents because she loved them both and did not want either of them to be alone. To make matters more painful for her she did not want to be away from either parent. For the child the separation pain manifested itself as hurt, feelings of not being wanted, anger at being prevented from having what she wanted, and guilt at what she perceived to be her role in the loss of a parent.

So the result was that there was a lot of anger and unhappiness in the family and Laura tried to keep her parents with her, by protesting at what was happening. She made her protest at the separation in a way that was impossible to ignore. She began a campaign of non-co-operation in her life both at home and wherever her parents were with her. She hid from her parents, broke rules whenever she could and, in any way that she could, drew attention to the fact that she was unhappy with what was happening. Her protest was not directed at either of her parents, more at what was happening to her. Inevitably it was her parents who suffered the brunt of her anger and their interpretation was coloured by their own agendas. To both parents, Laura's behaviour was seen as something within herself and nothing to do with how their psychological contents were seeping into her world. When her behaviour became unmanageable they decided to look for help.

For her parents the most striking thing was the difference in Laura when she was in the therapy room whether she was alone with me or with them. And it was this that helped each person to acknowledge and own what was going on. Both parents needed support in what they were attempting to do and since they could not support each other, in the place they were at that time, they automatically looked to me. The danger in this was that support for one might, in the suspicion of their separation, be taken as my 'being on one side or the other'.

Laura needed to know that though her parents were not going to live in the same house they were going to survive and would be there for her. She needed to know that they were both in agreement about what they were doing and she needed to feel that they each accepted the other's life. This helped both parents to realise the importance of listening to and answering Laura's separation fears, and they found a way to support and accept what the other was doing though it was not what each personally wanted.

One of the most difficult issues for the adults in this and in all separations is the genuine difficulty both have in accepting and understanding the other's feelings and needs. To begin with each has his or her own needs which at a time of crisis and hurt is such a big picture that nothing else is allowed in. Also, each is mainly concerned with his or her own survival and in looking after personal needs will inevitably put the needs of the other partner second. In particular when people are coming from a place and a life in which they have helped, supported and considered each other, but are in the middle of a struggle for personal survival, there is intense inner conflict between what they felt was right in the past and what they feel they now have to do to survive. In Laura's case, though both parents had accepted the inevitability of separation, the mother did not want to separate but the father did. In effect all their behaviour was motivated by an unconscious but understandable self-interest. Although neither was happy to say it openly, and probably was not conscious of it, every element of their behaviour was aimed at achieving their own partic-ular outcome.

For both parents the issue that constellated their own unconscious issues and allowed them to see and own their own behaviour, was the realisation that what they were doing was also having an effect on their daughter. This was an important discovery, and it presented an opportunity to withdraw the adult issues from the child. While the child was affected by the issue of the parents, it was important for everybody that the parents took back their own issues. Firstly, it helped Laura to let go of her guilt and anxiety, and to focus on herself. This withdrawal of unconscious motives and needs brought the adults to a point where they had to accept and face their own situation, and to acknowledge that the other person had his/her own pain and hurt to go through. An important feeling for both adults in this story was that each felt 'right' was on his or her side, and by implication that the other person was in the wrong. This moral superiority was given approval through the support of family members and friends and while this support is essential for the individual it can inhibit the process of progressing to a position of mutual acknowledgement of hurt.

Getting to a point of mutual acknowledgement of hurt involved a process of acknowledging, admitting and owning in a positive way, individual hurt and pain, and taking back the attribution of wrong to the other. For each to hear the other and listen to the other's story without wanting to influence it, given that they each had opposing survival needs, was helped by the realisation that Laura's needs were systemically influenced by how they each dealt with their own issues.

The mutual acknowledgement of hurt and 'right' was instrumental in taking the hostility and desire for revenge out of the situation. This desire for revenge, which manifests itself as wanting to hurt, to somehow 'do to you what you did to me', was being contained and carried unconsciously by the child. It was the mutual acknowledgement of hurt that enabled both to take back from the child their desire to hurt.

Laura inadvertently found herself in the centre of her parents' separation. She played a significant role in the healing process and in doing so helped her own case. The single most important aspect of this separation was the mutual acknowledgement of hurt by both adults, and it was this that brought them to a point where they could each allow the other to get on with life.

11

COMPETITION, GREED AND PERFECTION

One of the most fundamental dilemmas for the individual in society is the continuous inner battle between selflessness and greed, between competition and cooperation, between the needs of the individual and the needs of the collective. On the one hand there is in each of us both a need and an instinct to survive and to preserve ourselves as individuals even though this may be at the expense of others. This instinct for self-preservation manifests itself from the moment of birth through wanting our own way, fighting our corner, bullying others and putting ourselves first. If this instinct were to be given free rein, as it sometimes is, we would become totally self-centred, isolated and emotionally and socially crippled. On the other hand there is the other-centred, altruistic and collective-oriented side of the person which is more concerned with the needs and welfare of the outside world. This side of the person is connected to the need for belonging and the need for other affirmation in our lives. It fulfils our need for connection, contact and approval. If this aspect of ourselves were to be given free rein, and allowed to become totally unconscious, it would mean a total subjugation of the self to the needs of the society. The individual would be completely neglected and insignificant and would end up emotionally and socially ineffective. Complete selfishness and complete selflessness have the same consequences. The individual becomes emotionally helpless, personally isolated and socially alienated. To adapt and to survive and to reach the level of personal development that we term individuation, where people are at ease with who they are, can accept the good and bad about themselves, and can live on reasonable terms with themselves and with the world around them, they need a balance of selfishness and selflessness.

COMPETITION

The need to compete is inherent in the human psyche and forms an important part of the person's survival skills. Based on our instinctual will to survive and our need to protect our own self above everything else, the competitive instinct is always present in the psychological make-up of the person. For much of the time it is not exposed and the person may not be aware of its presence and power. Without the ability to compete we would not be able to survive and we would be at the mercy of our environment. The complete absence of the competitive instinct would leave us totally passive victims in a world where survival for the individual demands that we are able to stand up for ourselves against the demands of the collective needs of society. The competitive skill enables us to establish a balance between the demands of the outer world and our own needs.

However, the over-development of the competitive instinct and the over-valuing of competition by society has effects that are similarly damaging to both the individual and the society in which he or she lives. This is the situation that exists in our world today where there is an over-valuing of competition in our collective psyche. The mixture of the need to survive and the need to challenge our environment constitutes our competitive instinct and becomes exaggerated where competition is over-developed. It results in individuals or society being driven by an exaggerated sense of needing to prove that they are as good as, or better than, the other person. This is the constellation of unconscious feelings of inferiority.

COMPETITION AT WORK

In the world of work, business and commerce this exaggerated need to prove oneself manifests itself as a greed that can never be satisfied and that represents an unconscious, chronic dissatisfaction with self. In this situation the individual is driven by a need that cannot be satisfied, because it is a need that is not reflective of the inner reality of the self. This happens where the needs of the self, the inner need for balance and self-acceptance, is dominated and extinguished by the greed of the false self.

Such a need cannot be satisfied by accumulating material wealth, and the more wealth that is acquired the more the need is stimulated. The individual strives to satisfy this need by acting out of the over-developed masculine need to provide, to achieve, and to be superior. This greed is self-perpetuating because it is rooted in a deep emotional inadequacy which can never be met by the pursuit of material gain. The more we attempt to satisfy a need that is unsatisfiable, the more unhappy we become. The more we pursue a material satisfaction or an emotional need the more the inner dissatisfaction grows.

This underlying chronic feeling of unhappiness and dissatisfaction manifests itself as a mixture of restlessness and desire for immediate gratification, and an inability to relax because there is an unexplained compulsion to have it all now. It results in the way in which society and the individuals in it are always in a hurry. Everything is needed now, and an inherent impatience, fuelled by technological development, has taken hold.

The combination of innate competitive drives, the need to be better, the perceived need to be on top of the pile, in tandem with the development of technology, has led to a greater ability to have what we want, more quickly. The instant replay of sporting action on television, the immediate feedback from the play station, the high-speed communication of information, has created an expectation that we can have whatever we want, now; that we don't have to wait. There is also the implicit message that waiting, patience and deferred gratification are somehow not desirable.

This mix of ready availability, inner emotional greed and over-developed competitive instincts has allowed us to think that quicker is better, and that the end result, or the product, is much more important than the process of achieving it.

Such unconscious emotional dissatisfaction, and our desire to satisfy it through material acquisition as quickly as possible, has created a way of living our lives that is more about doing than being. Much of our lives is given over to doing and there is no time left to be a person.

COMPETITION IN SPORT

Competition, while it is a necessary tool in our emotional and social survival kit, can become over-developed and hence a destructive force in our lives. Sport provides us with a vehicle to satisfy our competitive needs in a way that is positive, healthy and satisfying and in a way that is not damaging to the individual or to others.

It is a vehicle meant to enable us to exercise the innate competitive skill, and to help us develop it to the level we need to survive in our world. The essence of the sporting relationship is the recognition of otherness and other-importance, the implicit acceptance of the validity of the other person's needs, while still being able to maintain one's own personal, emotional and psychological integrity. It is the ability to hold the conflictual middle ground where the individual is safe and the other person is safe.

Sport is also intended to be recreational and enjoyable and fun. The over-developed competitive instinct manifests itself in the way society has caused a contamination of the essential value of sport and has brought the work ethic into the play arena of sport. The result is that the recreational, therapeutic, and health value of sport has been lost. The cooperative, holding and healing value in sport has been replaced by the over-competitive, oppositional and subjugating values of greed and selfishness.

COMPETITION IN EDUCATION

Competition is mostly associated with sport and business, but it manifests itself in many other aspects of our lives. Much of our education system has a competitive aspect to it, where the process that the child goes through in school is dominated by the product of a place in college.

Providing opportunities for individuals to develop their ambition, while at the same time making sure that the system provides for the development of the whole person in a way that reflects and promotes a cooperative and other-oriented approach to life, is the challenge for our society.

Where the product becomes more important than the process of education, where the examination results become an end in themselves, or where we become overly concerned with measuring performance against objective criteria, the result is that children become objects in the system and the appearance of the system is more important than the development of the child. The crucial element in all of this is the expectation of the parents, the school and society. Where these expectations reflect only the collective needs of society, where the expectations are based on the unfulfilled ambitions of the school or parents, or where the expectations are not tied in to the particular needs of the child, the child becomes a vehicle for the expression of another's philosophy. The use of criteria that are competitive and reflect economic rather than humanistic values, turns the school into a factory that produces results rather than a process that develops the whole child. Eliminating the competitive ethos from the school would mean turning it into a creative, facilitating space where the needs of the child would be the guiding principle. Getting the balance right between the school as an agent of change in society and the school as a maintainer of the status quo, would mean that the school would influence society more than reflect it.

COMPETING IN APPEARANCE

Another manifestation of greed and of over-developed competition in our world is the way in which body image, shape and physical attractiveness have become measures of success and likeability. The intrusion of the corporate value system into the home has brought with it a spurious need to conform, through wearing designer clothes, having the perfect body shape, and having all the latest technological toys. Young people are drawn into a compliant pattern of standardised behaviour through a combination of powerful media messages, their growing dependence on technology, and the natural desire to belong to their peer group and be independent of their parents. This is an invasion of the person's need to belong, where the young person's need to be part of a peer world is taken over and disseminated as having to follow the herd. Being different is seen as being less.

The susceptibility of adolescents in particular, and of their parents to a lesser extent, to the pressure to look good, to appear attractive and to fit into the standard design, turns the person into an object. This objectification of the person, accelerated by the pressure to conform to the universal ideal of perfection, brutalises the humanity of people and turns them into a commodity.

ADDICTION

Addiction is a less obvious form of over-developed competition. The most damaging aspect of addiction is that in becoming addicted to a substance, a behaviour, or any aspect of life, we are giving over control of our lives to something outside of ourselves. As we have seen throughout this book the essence of healthy living is knowing ourselves, being able to have control over our lives and our environment, while being aware of the needs of those who are part of our world.

The underlying and unexpressed root of addiction is an unconscious and unacknowledged dissatisfaction within people themselves. It is an unhappiness with who they are and what they think they can be. It is not just that they are currently unhappy but also that there is an unhappiness with who they think they are going to be. This unhappiness is continually set against the standard of the perfect other, with whom they must compete, to be what they can be satisfied with.

The pressure on young people in particular to appear right, as seen in the pressure to wear particular clothes, the pressure to be the right shape, and the pressure to conform to the designer standard, are examples of the way in which the healthy and useful competitive instinct has been hijacked and brutalised by the application of the corporate core value of 'more is better'.

Because this unhappiness is unconscious and unacknowledged, individuals will not be aware of its existence and because it is a negative, painful aspect to their make-up, they will do everything they can to resist coming face to face with it. When I find something which has a combination of usefulness, accessibility and effectiveness in hiding the negative effect associated with my self-dissatisfaction, I will resort to this form of behaviour more and more. The more I engage in this avoidance behaviour and the more 'successful' it seems to be, the more it becomes part of my psychological survival package. When the behaviour becomes so assimilated into my overall way of being that I need it, that I think I cannot survive without it, I am now dependent. On the surface, this dependency seems like a healthy situation and I feel comfortable in it and am convinced that everything is fine because I am not conscious of any dissatisfaction with who I am. But the negative side of the dependency is that it is based on my own unwillingness to face the dissatisfaction that I have within me, and which unless dealt with through bringing it to consciousness, will continue to block my personal growth and development.

ADDICTION TO PERFECTION

Our need for order in life, an order that is necessary to take care of our achievement needs and our satisfaction needs, is one of the growth conditions for the addiction to perfection. Our desire to please others through conforming to accepted ways of dress, material possessions and the way in which we allow our expectations for children to be driven by outside social factors, all help to fulfil our need to belong but also have the potential to facilitate the development of an addiction to perfection.

Addiction to perfection manifests itself in the form of an over-zealousness in regard to hygiene, an over-concern for order and neatness and an over-anxiety about physical appearance, bodily shape and dressing. These 'overs' are based on a healthy need for looking after ourselves that has been allowed to get out of control, and they can be directed towards ourselves, our children or our family.

Addiction to perfection in the material, physical sense of clothes, body, or possessions is often in direct proportion to the level of unhappiness with the inner self. The greater the inner, unconscious self-dissatisfaction, the more the need to have perfection in the outer, personal environment.

ADDICTION TO WORK

Addiction to what is primarily a good, useful and necessary pursuit can have negative consequences. Because of the value of work in the development of our personal and social esteem, and because of its importance in our survival, addiction to work is a convenient and easily developed refuge for those of us who are unable to confront our own shadow. The inherent danger in all of the positive aspects of our lives is that in engaging positively in these activities we can become too taken up with the positivity of the activity, allow ourselves to be controlled by it and gradually become taken over by it. Apart from becoming over-involved through being attracted to it, we may also become over-involved as a means of avoiding negative aspects in our own personal world. Over-involvement in any one area of our lives inevitably means under-involvement in another. If we spend too much time at work, if we spend too much time thinking about work, or if we use our work to escape from unpleasant aspects of our lives, we will inevitably neglect other areas of our being and existence. In the case of work, because it is so important in our world, so necessary for both material and emotional satisfaction, and has such a positive dimension to it, it is one of the easiest to become addicted to.

We model this positive work attitude to our children, we have a negative perception of those who don't work, and we need work for the individual and collective good. So work is seen as a good thing in our lives. Because it is so good, so necessary and so valuable we rarely find fault with the person who spends too much time at work.

Material advantage is usually synonymous with educational, social and personal success, and it is usually seen as desirable for a person to work harder than his neighbour or his colleague or his brother. Over-working is rewarded materially and this makes it seem beneficial and allows us to overlook the negative aspects.

The make-up of the person is also a factor in the predilection to over-working. The person whose dominant function is logic and thinking, who is left brain dominant and whose less-used function is feeling and the creative right side of the brain, will be more likely to be sucked in by the attractions of over-working. These personality traits which are so necessary for the survival of the person make it very easy for people who are more thinking than feeling, more logical than intuitive, to overwork.

Over-working has become almost accepted practice in a world view that is dominated by academic achievement, ambition, parental hot-housing of children, and immediate gratification fuelled by the media message that material possessions and image are desirable goals in themselves, and are the key to personal happiness.

ADDICTION TO DISTRACTION

A similar form of addiction which has become prevalent in our lives is a form of always having something to do, the addiction to distraction. This often begins in a family where the children are always assigned tasks, and their lives are structured and supervised to the degree that they are never allowed to be alone, to daydream or to do anything without the parent having an input. Such an attitude comes from the idea that children will get into trouble if they have nothing useful to do, and that it is therefore necessary for parents to ensure that their children always have something useful to do. This addiction to distraction broadens to include always having noise in the background, never being alone, always having the television on, and results in a life where there is never space to be with oneself. The dependency becomes so deeply rooted that the withdrawal of the crutch of distraction leads to an inability to cope and a breakdown of the life systems.

The ability to be on our own with ourselves is central to dealing with addictions. It is, for the most part, our fear of our inner dissatisfaction that prevents us from being with ourselves.

Signs of being overly competitive:

➤ Always wanting to have the last word
➤ Interrupting when someone is speaking
➤ Being annoyed by the success of others
➤ Impatience with mistakes
➤ Pointing the index finger at the person being addressed
➤ Being overly concerned with order and neatness
➤ Finding it difficult to allow others to have a say
➤ Always wanting more
➤ Inability to sit quietly with nothing to do
➤ Impatience when others are speaking

A FAMILY STORY

John and Jean have four children who are all schoolgoing. Both parents work outside the home and are successful in what they do. Their children are doing well at school, and have inherited their parents' achievement values. There is a strong family ethic of competition, ambition and being the best. This shows in the overt ways of wanting the children to do well at school.

Although the children live within walking distance of the school, they are driven to school and collected from school. After school they attend music lessons, swimming and drama classes. This entails a continuation of the adult supervision that is a part of their school day. During the summer holidays the children attend summer camps.

The children's day is so structured and organised that they never have time to be by themselves. Everything they do is supervised by an adult so that they always have an adult to consult with and to depend on when things go wrong. Consequently they have very little opportunity to develop and practise skills of negotiation, argument and conflict resolution. Because they are not allowed to walk to school they miss out on opportunities to socialise, to develop the ability to survive in the emotional rough and tumble of children's banter. The school playground is also supervised so there is limited opportunity for them to develop healthy social skills.

One of the features of this family is the limited personal contact between them. Because both parents follow successful careers, and because the children are part of so many structured after-school activities, there is little time for one-to-one personal contact. Much of the contact is by mobile phone, e-mail and notes left on the kitchen table. This has effects for both parents and children.

Because of the continued supervision of the children's lives and because of the children's involvement in organised activities, they have no time to be by themselves. The unconscious message from the parents' lifestyle is that unless the activity is structured, useful and has a measurable result, it is a waste of time. The parents live very full lives and have no time to be, no time to spend 'doing nothing', and this message is transmitted consciously and unconsciously to the children.

The family came to see me to address the problem of one of their children being bullied. Although this was the presenting problem, and it was very real and immediate, having spent some time with parents and child separately, we decided to work with the family as a group and to approach the bullying from a systemic viewpoint. This meant addressing many issues that initially the parents felt had nothing to do with the reason they came to see me.

It was difficult for the parents to work with the idea that they were in some way part of what was happening to their child outside of the home.

We began in a full family session by talking about the position, role and status of each person in the family system. This allowed each person to see the way in which the six individuals were connected emotionally, behaviourally, and spatially. The behaviour of any one person had an effect on all the others in the family to a greater or lesser degree. The degree of influence was determined by the perception each of the others had of the individual.

As we explored this issue more and more each of the family members, and particularly the parents, began to realise that each person in the family had a different status and a different level of influence. They realised that, unconsciously, each of the children was being treated in a different way. It became clear that the child who was being bullied was the one who had very little say in what happened within the family system. The only influence he had was achieved through being passive and agreeable and by being a good boy. This powerful compliance was effective in giving him status within the family but it was also making him more susceptible to being controlled in the outside world which was much more competitive.

This family was a successful family, and the work ethic was very important. In addition it was considered important that each person could look after himself or herself. There was little time for weakness, or for not being able to cope. Within this type of system it was very difficult for the parents to see what was happening, particularly since they did not want to see it. The family was so busy with life and with doing things that they failed to notice that one member was finding it difficult to keep up with what was expected of him. In fact they paid little or no attention to any of the children and in this sense the child who was being bullied was doing the whole family a favour. By being unable to cope he was forcing the family to take notice of what was going on within it.

The boy's personality and overall psychological make-up contributed in no small way to what was happening. Being a good boy meant achieving high grades at school, never stepping out of line and always doing what he was told. He had become so good at being a good boy that there was an expectation that he would always be a good boy, and if he stood up for himself or behaved assertively this would be stepping out of the stereotype the others had created for him. It would cause the other members of the family to put him down. This good compliant behaviour made him an easy subject to be bottom of the pecking order in the family, and an easy target in the competitive world of the playground and the street.

What was being modelled to this boy was a system where he had no say, where he allowed others to make decisions for him and where he was afraid to speak up for himself. This was the way of being which was being held out to him and with which he was beginning to feel satisfied. The more he adopted this way of orienting himself to the outside world, the more comfortable he became within it and the less he stood out within his family. The child naturally took this 'model of a successful way of being' with him out into the world.

So the bullying outside the home was actually a 'good thing' for the family, provided they did something about it.

It was important that all members of the family felt a part of what we were doing, and this was in essence the issue that had to be addressed, in the wider reality of the family and society. It was a matter of consciousness and inclusion. By talking about the relationship dynamics of the family and allowing everyone to see the role that each was playing, how each of them was affected by the others in the group, we were able to begin the process of changing what was happening.

The family, by engaging in a process of therapy, were beginning to do the things they needed to do in reality. This included listening to each other, talking to each other, and taking note of the needs of the others in the group. The therapy sessions became the model for group behaviour in real life and everybody was able to see that there was another way of being to the one they had experience of.

The difficulties experienced in working towards the idea of collective awareness and collective responsibility were in themselves symbolic of the family's unwillingness to see themselves individually, as part of the wider psychological sphere of influence of what was happening to other members of the group. By looking at this particular issue in conjunction with the work we did on role and status with each person in the family, we were able to focus attention on the fact that what happened to one member of the group affected the others, whether it was negative or positive. Where one member of the family was over-compliant and passive this was affecting the others, because it meant that their power and influence within the group was proportionately increased. Because it was increased at the expense of another member of the group it meant that the family as a whole was not functioning as well as it could.

There was a feeling for the parents that spending time in this way was somehow not productive and perhaps even a waste of time. Again we were able to take this point and see how it applied in reality within the family. It reflected the way in which the family were so busy doing, achieving and competing to have everything right, that there was no time to reflect, to take stock, and to 'be'. By addressing the parents' difficulty with this idea within the therapy setting, we were able to place it back in the real world of the family's life together.

12

WORK AND PLAY

The compulsive drive for success, achievement and material
gain has brought about a significant shift in the way in which
society as a whole and people individually live their lives.
Achieving a satisfactory life state requires each of us, as separate
individuals, and as members of the collective world of society as a
whole, to have a balance of play and work in our lives. The work
aspect of our lives provides us with the much needed life satisfaction that comes from achievement, doing, being valued and
contributing to our community and society. This translates as self-
worth and gives us the feeling that we are valuable and valued. To
be able to play our part in the world of work requires not only
physical energy but also psychological and emotional energy. This
type of energy is generated in a number of ways.

Through working in our community, contributing in the
workplace, providing for our material needs and taking care of our
family we gain satisfaction, a feeling of being needed, a sense of
our own individual worth, and the motivation to get up tomorrow and continue to engage in our work. In addition to this, we
may have what is known as 'job satisfaction' and this helps to give
us psychological and emotional energy to continue with our lives
and in particular with our work.

There is also, however, a basic human need in each person for
play, fun and recreation. This need is exercised by involvement in
all forms of sport, recreation, play, or any form of hobby that the
person enjoys. The basic currency of play is the idea of intrinsic
motivation. Intrinsic motivation is wanting to take part in an
activity purely for the enjoyment one gets from it; taking part in

an activity for its own sake. There is no monetary gain, no possibility of material gain and no need to compete with others or to feel that one has to meet any performance criteria to gain satisfaction. The need for relaxation is as basic and necessary as the need for achievement, and it is equally as important in the provision of energy, both physical and emotional, in the life of the person. Fun and work are the two balancing poles of life and it is by having a balance of these two that we achieve the state of internal equilibrium that is essential for healthy living.

One of the main outcomes from playing and having fun is a sense of friendship and companionship. This feeling of being liked and being included in the group satisfies our basic need to belong and to feel part of a system that is bigger and stronger than the individual. It helps to satisfy our need to feel safe, secure and protected. This need to belong can also be satisfied in some degree in the working environment, but in the context of recreation, play and enjoyment it has a more personal function. The feeling of belonging to a group which shares our interests, which actively invites us in, and which wants us because of who we are rather than what we are, is a feeling of being safe, a feeling of being valued, and a feeling of playing an active part in the wider world.

Having fun is also necessary so that the creative side of the brain is brought into play and we are enabled to feel that we are shaping and influencing our environment. The world of work for the most part is a world where the left side of the brain is used. It is a world where we have to call on those skills that are most associated with the logical side of the brain, which contains the ability to interpret, to speak, to read, to follow directions, and to deal with detail. These are the most commonly used aspects of our make-up as society in general is left-brain dominant and rewards thinking that is linear, logical, reality based and sequential. But, both for society and for the individual, if we confine our consciousness to the left side of the brain we are leaving half of our brain unused and undeveloped. The right side of the brain approaches the world in a holistic and intuitive way, and it is in this side of the brain that the skills associated with art, music, emotional expression and general creativity are housed. The world of play and fun provides us with opportunities to develop the right side of the brain, the creative side, the underused side. Achieving the balance between play and work, between fun and seriousness, means achieving a balance between any one part of the person and the whole person, between reality and fantasy, between the logical and the intuitive, between the thinking and the feeling, and between the verbal and non-verbal ways of communication.

Play and having fun are creative because they allow us to become absorbed in an activity for its own sake, without having to perform to please others. By becoming engrossed in a fun activity, the individual can switch off from the serious emotional, intellectual and social demands of work. The nature of work is that it is serious and important in our lives. We are paid for it, and this requires us to commit emotional and physical energy to it. It requires us to be conscious and aware of what we are doing and to focus intellectually. There is commitment, responsibility to others, seriousness and the sense that we have to do it. Therefore work uses up energy. It is demanding emotionally, physically and psychologically, and if we do not find the time to switch off from this level of involvement, there is an imbalance in our way of being that will eventually cause breakdown.

Part of the value of play is that it confers on us the permission to put aside our persona. It allows us to put aside the serious adult work side of our being, and to take on the playful, childlike and fun side of our personality. This fantasy side is present in all of us, but more and more it is being denied expression and therefore it is unused and undeveloped. The current preoccupation in society with performance, production and profit has displaced the fun element from our world.

Play is the best way to switch off from this high-powered activity and it has two functions in the process. It is not just our way of switching off from the demands of work, it is also the means of building up our energy levels again. It has a therapeutic and pragmatic function, in as much as it helps to dissipate the tensions and frustrations that build up during work and that we need to rid ourselves of. These negative tensions and stresses will be stored in our unconscious, hidden from our consciousness, unless we can legitimately deal with them through play and relaxation.

One of the difficulties that arises here is the feeling that having fun is somehow wasting time and this often makes it difficult for the person to let go of the work attitude. In learning to have fun in our lives we need to be able to live in the now, to be where we are at this time and not to be thinking of what we could be doing or should be doing. More and more of our lives is given to planning and preparing for what is going to happen, in a bid to be in control of our future world. This is a necessary part of living and surviving but there is a need to bring balance to this future orientation.

If, however, we become too concerned with being ready for tomorrow, if we always try to know what the future holds and if we try to be always in control of what is going to happen, our world will be dominated by the future. Where our world is dominated by anxiety about the future, our present world is absent and we have no opportunity to be where we are now and to enjoy what we are doing right now.

Tapping into the right side of the brain, and allowing ourselves to engage in play and relaxation, teaches us to be comfortable with uncertainty and to give expression to our creative, intuitive side. It is here that we find the balance for the serious demanding work side of our being, because it is in this area of our brain that we find our ability to enjoy music, to be creative in art, to invent, and to indulge that imaginative side of our being which is not valued in the world of work.

Being comfortable with uncertainty is important for our development as whole people, but it goes against the values of the planning, structured world of certainty which is the world of work. By tapping into our creative side and by allowing ourselves the opportunity to engage in activities that are unpredictable, we allow our psyche to take a rest from the strain of meeting deadlines, being ready for tomorrow and maintaining our work persona. The play and fun side of our psyche enables us to engage in activities which have uncertain outcomes and where the participation is more important than the outcome. A process-oriented approach to some aspects of life, where the participation, the engaging, the activity itself is the reason for our involvement in a particular activity, is necessary to counterbalance the work part of our world which is product orientated.

One of the concerns for today is the way in which the values of work have become a part of our sport and play. In the area of children's sport and play, it is partly due to the perceived dangers in allowing children to play by themselves. This has led to a gradual acceptance by society that children should not be left alone. The perception that it is not safe to let children play by themselves, and that therefore they should at all times be supervised, has led to changes in the nature of the play activity, and in the motive for play. Being watched at play takes away the free, imaginative and fantasy elements of the play activity. Knowing they are being watched puts a different motive into the play as the children feel they are doing it more for the people watching than for the sake of the activity itself. It is clear that children are playing less and less, and that the range of their games is being limited. There are many reason for this: lifestyle, increased usage of technology, and safety issues. Perhaps it is also the fact that there is not the same pleasure in playing when you are being watched.

The professionalisation of sport has implications for the way in which the values of the workplace have taken away from the recreational and therapeutic value of adult and child sport. While there are obvious reasons for the development of professional elite sport, the way in which the effects of this type of sport have begun to influence ordinary recreational sport needs to be addressed. The promotion of elite professional sport on television has had two major effects. It has made it easier for people to feel a part of sporting activity through virtual sport, and it has influenced the levels of participation in the actual playing of sport. The professional sport value system of product, results and measurable success has begun to influence ordinary, recreational, fun sport. The winning-is-everything attitude, so much a part of the corporate world, has invaded all levels of sporting activity.

The need here is for the individual to engage in sport and recreational activities that are based on fun, friendship and intrinsic motivation. If we take part in sport that is governed by the work-place value system, we are getting no respite from the pressure of work and we are not promoting the development of the creative, intuitive and imaginative side of ourselves.

Ask yourself these questions as you approach a game:

➤ Have I left my persona at home?
➤ Why am I playing this game?
➤ Have I time to talk to the people I am with?
➤ Are these the people I work with?
➤ Do I look forward to the experience?

PAUL'S STORY

When Paul was 18 he tried to escape the family business and make his own way in the world. The ties were so strong and he felt so guilty about leaving his parents on their own, that he was unable to do this. He took over the family business and that became his occupation. Later he married and the business was truly his family business. He had a natural ambition which helped him to do well and he quickly became successful.

But there was an underlying dissatisfaction with the importance and value of the work he was doing and with who he thought he was. He was unable to articulate this grandiosity and it remained unconscious until he became much older.

His work lent itself to the 'more is better' type of thinking, and the more time and energy he put into his work the better it seemed. As he became more successful, he was convinced that he was providing more and more for his children. Emotional nurturing was increasingly being confused with material provision. This positive work complex enabled him to spend more and more time at his work in the belief that the more work he did the better he was as a father and as a provider. His work was not only his occupation, it was his chief source of narcissistic supplies; so he was depending on his work for his sense of worth as a person, as a parent and as a husband. His work was also his chief way of achieving social esteem. It was through his business that he achieved overall fulfilment as a person.

But another pattern was emerging in his life. His work was his escape from any form of unpleasantness in his life. If he had an argument with one of his family he would hide his anger and resentment in his work. This was easy to do as work had such a positive place in his world. The pattern continued until it became his escape from the world. His way of dealing with any unpleasantness in his family life or in his social life was to go to work.

Paul had become dependent on work and it was a harmful dependency. There were many effects of this. Most obviously he became isolated from his family. He lost touch with the emotional world of his children, he was unable to connect with them, and they were unable to get into his world. The lines of communication were damaged to the extent that the only time there was any real communication was when there was disagreement between them. The growing unconscious resentment was shared by the children and both parents, each for their own particular reason. This resentment gradually turned to negative, abusive criticism on both sides, with Paul finding it difficult to see any good in his children and they in turn unable to see anything positive in their father. This overt emotional aggression was the constellation of inner frustration, hatred and mistrust which had developed because the children believed that Paul's work was more important than they were. Paul in turn believed that his children were hindering his chances of success.

There was an additional problem in all of this. Even though he was successful at his work, even though he spent so much time at work, and even though it was his main way of survival in the world,

Paul felt that the work he was doing was beneath him. This feeling manifested itself in other ways where he buried himself in grandiose schemes and ideas and dismissed any ordinary work or family pursuit as being of no value.

As the children grew to adolescence, the natural need for independence from their parents was contaminated by an underlying hatred and aggression towards Paul. Paul's inability to get close to and understand his children, and their desire to put emotional distance between themselves and their father, caused him to be uncomfortable and uneasy with them and to be embarrassed and ashamed of them in public. Although he tried to hide this and managed to do so outwardly, the shame and embarrassment was strongly felt by the children and their reaction was to repeat the behaviour that had been modelled to them. They were more and more drawn to home because the less emotional nurturing they received the more they needed. Yet the more time they spent at home the more hostility and isolation they felt. They were frustrated and confused and took out their aggression on anyone at home. This behaviour was not repeated when they were outside where they tended to become loners, unable to give the necessary trust and acceptance to become members of groups. Since they were receiving negative emotional feedback outside the family, they more and more sought the nurture they needed at home.

Somebody needed to break the tightly knit circle of emotional aggression, and given that Paul was the most powerful player in this game it had to be he. The process of acknowledging his part in all of this was difficult and painful for Paul and it was only after spending many sessions putting the blame on to other members of his family, realising that no matter where he looked the trail always came back to him, that Paul was able to see the painful road that lay ahead.

The biggest issue in all this work was to counter Paul's self-blame and his desire to beat himself up. Left alone he was likely to put all the hatred and aggression which he had been directing to others, on to himself. He was in danger of thinking corporatively and believing that the only solution was to pay his children back by doing to himself what he had been doing to them. However, we worked towards a view of himself that was accepting and tolerant and that also would enable him to acknowledge what had happened, accept the seriousness of it and own his own behaviour. It would then be possible for him to break the circle of aggression. While doing this he had to allow the children to exercise their right to their feelings towards him and to the desire to 'get their own back' and yet be able to hold their aggression as a parent does with an infant.

Intellectualisation was a constant companion in all of this and we had to be conscious of the risk that talking about it was enough. The talk was a necessary initial stage in the process of healing Paul's own damaged self-view. It was only by doing this that he could begin to see and accept the real people within his children.

13

ANGER

Dealing with anger and its close relative, aggression, is an important part of being able to cope with life. For the most part anger is seen as a negative emotion and one which society tells us should be kept hidden, should not be expressed. This view is due to our in-built fear of confrontation and the unpleasant feelings and discomfort that anger brings up in us. It is also due to our fear that if we are allowed to express anger openly and freely, it will lead to aggression and violence. However, by repressing our anger, we turn it in on ourselves and it becomes a part of our internal matrix of behaviour, feelings and motives. The anger, though unexpressed, is nonetheless active within us and becomes a very strong influence on the way in which we orient ourselves to the world around us. It shapes our behaviour and becomes an invisible filter through which our perception of the world around us is formed. If we have unexpressed or unacknowledged anger within us it will be manifested unconsciously in the way we perceive others in our world, the way we relate to others in our world and the way we treat others in our world.

Internalised, unexpressed anger grows within us. The longer it remains repressed and unacknowledged, the deeper it is forced into our unconscious and the more destructive and damaging it becomes. Because our anger is so painful to face, and so potentially destructive, we run away from it or hide it, but the more we hide it the more frightening it becomes. Though it is repressed and unacknowledged, our anger is still alive and being expressed unconsciously, in ways that we are not aware of. The worst place for anger is within. While it is kept hidden it is still active and operational and therefore influencing the behaviour of the person. The effects of unexpressed anger are self-hate, low self-esteem and an inability to accept others.

Unacknowledged anger is expressed unconsciously through:

➤ begrudgery
➤ negativity
➤ difficulty in accepting the positives in the world around us
➤ being over-critical
➤ bitterness towards other people
➤ over-competitiveness
➤ taking things too personally
➤ difficulty in liking other people
➤ spontaneous negative reaction to people, ideas, events
➤ outbursts of anger and aggression
➤ wanting to hurt others, verbally, physically, emotionally.

Dealing with anger presents difficulties because to do so we have to recognise it for what it is: a strong feeling of having been wronged and wanting to avenge that feeling. Our anger may be based in some actual wrong that has been done to us, or it may be that we wrongly perceive that a wrong has been done to us. It may be based in a relationship with someone who is valuable to us and this can make it difficult to admit the source of our anger. But, though we may not be aware of the real source of our anger, it is there, it is ours and we are at the mercy of its power, unless we do something about it.

Where we are unable to recognise the source of the anger, where we are unable to acknowledge the anger itself, we tend to project the anger and the blame for the anger on to another person. This projection of our anger has two effects. Firstly it means that unless we are able to withdraw the projection from the other person we are unable to deal with it in ourselves. Because projection is an unconscious process we are unaware that the person we feel anger towards may not be the actual cause of our anger. It is much less painful to live with if we 'think' that the other person is responsible for our unhappiness. The second aspect of this is that it affects our relationships at work, at home, and in society generally. We think that if we can't see our anger, then it does not exist, and that it is not part of the psychological content of our environment. This shows itself in the behaviour of the person whose attitudes and reactions indicate that he is angry but who insists that he is not angry. As long as it remains unconscious nothing will change.

REVENGE

It is this simmering, resentful anger that can turn into overt physical, emotional or behavioural aggression towards another person in an attempt to restore the emotional equilibrium which we feel has been damaged. The need for revenge stems from a deep feeling of having been damaged and diminished by the behaviour of another, and which seeks restoration through getting back at the reason for our injury. Our inner sense of justice requires us to take action to restore our self-view by giving back the hurt that has been given to us. We are driven by the need to reassert the integrity of our inner being which we feel has been fragmented by the hurt of another. The disintegration and damage to our emotional integrity demands that we ourselves do something to restore the wholeness of the self, and that unless we take it on in an honest way, our self-respect suffers.

Usually both the original hurt and the need for revenge are hidden from our conscious awareness, and unless we do something about becoming aware of why we are behaving the way we are, it will take control of us and become unmanageable. Revenge is strongly related to anger, hostility and feelings of being unfairly treated. Given the right set of circumstances we all have the capability, the potential and the need to look for revenge. It is born out of our innate need and instinct to survive in a way that satisfies our view of ourselves in the world and our sense of being wronged. There is a part of our make-up which demands that, when we feel that our integrity as a human being has been damaged, or when our self-view has been threatened, we need to bring our sense of self back to a point where we can live with it. The need for revenge is rooted in the feeling that somebody or something out there has wronged us and that our inner balance can only be restored by seeing that person or thing suffer in the same way that we have suffered.

Our desire for getting our own back shows itself in many areas of our lives and we often see that there is a gap between what we say we want to do and what we are actually doing. We can see this in situations such as marital separation where there is verbal commitment to acceptance and moving forward, but the hurt remains unexpressed and blocks the flow of the creative, positive energy needed for healing and growth.

DEALING WITH ANGER AND REVENGE

➤ Being on friendly terms with our anger is an important and healthy ingredient of anger management. We are conditioned to have a negative feeling towards anger, to resist it and to try to repress it because we see it as being such a destructive element in our make-up. The effects of uncontrolled anger are damaging to ourselves and to those in our world. In order to be able to deal with our anger and the anger of others in our lives, it is helpful if we can treat it as a real part of our make-up which is present whether we like it or not. In trying to come to terms with our anger, we are setting out to have control over it, rather than allowing it to control us. Acknowledging and owning it is the first step to taking away the power it has over us and then when we have control of it we can change it.

➤ Identifying the real source of the anger is an important part of the process of dealing with our anger. Often we are unaware of the real source of the anger we are expressing, and we may be projecting feelings of anger on to a person who is not really the cause of our anger. To identify the source of our anger, we need to sit with it, accept it as a part of our world at this particular time, and allow ourselves the time and space to tune in to our unconscious world. This helps us to deal with the clouding effect of the ego which will attribute blame externally to avoid having to face up to its own negative side.

➤ In developing the power to manage our anger and to keep it from being a negative, damaging part of ourselves, it is important that we are able to own it. Owning our anger means that we can acknowledge that it is ours, that it is our own responsibility and that we cannot attribute it to others in our lives. This owning of a negative side of ourselves is an inescapable step in the process of taking responsibility for our own lives.

➤ Being able to give expression to anger without damaging ourselves or others is an important aspect in the process of dealing with anger. If we keep anger hidden or repressed it is internalised and turned against the self. This leads to low self-esteem and causes us to feel that for a reason unknown, in fact for no real reason, we should be punished. It is therefore much more healthy if the anger can be 'put out' into the environment. If the anger is rightfully directed at another person it should be expressed in a way that is honest, honours the integrity of the individual, and is not threatening to the other person. By putting the anger out, we are respecting our own selves and at the same time putting it where it belongs. By hiding or repressing it we are keeping it within ourselves and this leads to feelings of shame and resentment towards ourselves and towards the 'rightful owner' of the anger.

➤ The ability to be angry and the willingness to allow ourselves to be angry are important in the overall picture of anger management. Often adults feel that their anger should not be externalised in front of children and that it is better to wait until children are in bed or out of the room. Children can sense the anger even if it is not expressed openly, and may wrongly feel that they are the cause. This postponing of anger also unconsciously transmits to children the idea that they should contain their anger and keep it hidden rather than get it out.

Coping with the feeling of revenge in a way that is satisfying to ourselves and yet does not harm the object of our feeling, again revolves around bringing to consciousness issues that we may be afraid to face.

➤ We can't deal with it unless we acknowledge its existence within us. This involves admitting that it is there, that it is part of us, and that it is alright for us to feel like this.
➤ If we can acknowledge the existence of the feeling we can then move to a point where we can own it. Ownership of negative feelings is always difficult because it means thinking badly of ourselves. In this situation it is helpful if we can view the idea of revenge and the desire for revenge as normal aspects of the human psyche. If we view them as negative, bad and destructive we will tend to repress them, hide them in our unconscious, and be reluctant to deal with them.
➤ The feeling of wanting revenge is in itself not the problem, it is what we do with this feeling that is important. The reason society in general shies away from discussing it, and the reason we avoid it in our own lives, is because the consequences of acting out our feeling of revenge are too serious a risk. If we can acknowledge its existence and own the feeling, then we can begin to deal with the issue.
➤ By taking ownership we are also taking control of and responsibility for our feeling, whereas if we leave the feeling of revenge in our unconscious we allow ourselves to be in its control.
➤ When we make conscious the feeling of revenge we can then ask ourselves a number of questions:
  − Is this feeling genuine?
  − Did this person really do this to me?
  − Is the feeling mine, not someone else's?
  − Did the person intend to hurt me?

- How much responsibility is mine?
- What are the consequences of acting out my feeling of revenge?
- The feeling of revenge is in me; is the healing also in me?
- Can I talk to the person in question?

JAMES' STORY

James is a man in his fifties who in almost all aspects of his life is happy. He is happy with who he is, with his work, with his family and with himself. When he came to see me he had 'only one problem', and this he described as his blackness. He told how, at certain times and for no reason that he was conscious of, he would be assailed by fears, doubts, anxieties and worries. He would suddenly be taken over by dark fears about himself and his family which he knew, at a logical level, were unfounded, but which he nevertheless was unable to get out of.

When he was in the grip of these fears he felt totally controlled by them and became completely immobilised and unable to function at work or at home. He had become obsessed with this blackness and he felt that he could never be completely happy until he got a 'cure' for it. He came to me having tried medication and various other forms of treatment, and also expecting a particular way of dealing with it.

The work with James shows us a number of important issues:

➤ It shows that we can take control of issues in our life that seem to control us.
➤ It shows how the process of change is the responsibility of the person, not the therapist.
➤ It shows the importance of handing this responsibility to the person.
➤ It shows that the work of therapy is concerned with the person as a whole and not just with the pathology or presenting problem.

Addressing James' expectations about the therapy process was the starting point. This was part of the wider issue of having preconceived

notions about people and the world, why we are under the influence
of preconceived notions and what to do about this. But the narrow
issue here was James' expectations about me in particular and the
process in general. He had come with a particular view of who I was,
how I worked and what I would do to him.

Part of the early sessions addressed the question of James' expectation that it was the therapist who would bring the change. It was
essential that the equalisation process was initiated and that James
could work with the idea that it was he who would bring about
change in his life. This was part of a wider issue of power within the
therapy room, and a handing back by me of the power of change to
James. As in other cases it involved a risk, as James had come to me
with the preconceived notion that I was the doctor and that I had the
special power of knowledge that would cure him. We explored the
idea of facilitation, where I was not losing any status in either my own
eyes or in James' eyes, but was happy with the status of partnership
within the creative space of the therapy process. It was a shared space
in time and in experience, and the guiding principle for the process
tended to be the particular psychological package that James brought
to each weekly session. We moved to a position where we accepted
that we were working together and would both change as a result.

We progressed this by agreeing that I could not know in advance
how we would work, what approach we would take, or how he
would respond to this. We could not plan a therapy process without
knowing who James was, what he would bring to the process and
how these contents would impact. This meant that there would be a
potentiality and a possibility and an openness of mind in regard to
each particular session, and we would be guided by the principle that
whatever was happening in James' world at the particular time was
the issue that needed to be addressed. This would also be influenced
by what was happening in my world at that time.

Dealing with the 'it' in James' story was an important part of the
whole process, and we had to address this early on. James felt that his
blackness, his fears, and his anxieties were something that could be
dealt with in a logical, confrontational way. He felt that this was

something that was not part of him but was an externally imposed condition that he did not own, that he had no control over and that he had no responsibility for. What we hoped to do here was to change the 'it' to 'me', and in the process allow James change his self-view so that he could include his darkness, his shadow, in his overall view of himself. If he could accept that his shadow was part of him and not something outside of him we could begin the process of befriending and controlling it.

At the beginning of our work together James was being controlled by his shadow and this was caused by:

➤ not accepting it as part of him
➤ continually fighting it
➤ believing it to be outside of him
➤ not taking responsibility for it.

Taking control and responsibility for his blackness was crucial to James' empowering and equalisation in the therapy process. In doing this he was making a statement of power to himself, and he was shedding his fear of his shadow. It led to a cessation of hostilities towards his blackness and allowed the befriending process to begin. For James this was unthinkable at the start. It seemed that to befriend something that had persecuted him for years was the very opposite to what he should be doing. The masculine in him wanted to fight something that he believed to be his enemy and that he hated. It was revealing to James himself, when he realised that the only area of his life where he exercised this masculine fighting complex was towards part of himself. He saw that he was not doing it in the outer world. By acknowledging and accepting his shadow as an integral part of himself he was effectively taking control of it, and this helped him to see that while his blackness was a part of him and would always be there in some respects, it was his and he could have a say in how he was affected by it.

Honouring the masculine principle was an important part of James' life. He was uncomfortable with the idea of expressing anger openly, challenging others, or criticising in the outer world, and it was the realisation that he was doing this against himself that helped to bring to consciousness his neglect of this important masculine behaviour. Hand-in-hand with this raised consciousness was the withdrawal of his hostility towards that part of himself that he did not like. His oppositional defiance of the blackness was in fact giving it energy and influence, and by withdrawing his aggression towards it he took energy away from it, and lessened its influence in his life.

14

FINDING THE
BALANCE

.‿

Many difficulties in life arise in the context of achieving a balance between knowing our capabilities and our limits. It is often because we are expected to do something which is beyond our capacity, or because we believe that we cannot do something which is within our capacity that we find ourselves in difficulties. The balance between 'can' and 'can't' and more importantly the acceptance of this reality in our lives is crucial to being effective in our world. Many of our frustrations and fears are generated by the inability to accept that it is allowable not to be able to do some things, and that it is also allowable to try in the hope that we may succeed. This willingness to try and the confidence to fail are essential characteristics of people who are at ease with themselves.

Central to the whole idea of balance is self-knowledge and self-awareness. We all ask ourselves: Who am I? What can I do? What can I not do? Self-knowledge enables us to answer these questions and to either accept what we find or to do what we can to change the situation. Self-awareness enables us to know, accept and work with the good and the bad, the positive and the negative, the masculine and the feminine. It allows us to be aware of all aspects of our make-up, to take ownership of these and to integrate them in a way that helps us to express, and be confident about ourselves in a holistic way.

Finding the balance between the masculine and the feminine within our overall make-up, and being able to express this in a way that presents us as integrated and attractive individuals to the outer world, is fundamental to our finding a way of being with which we can be reasonably satisfied. If the masculine aspects of our make-up are too evident and over-developed, then we are hostile and aggressive, and we lose out on belonging relationships and companionship. If our feminine principle is too developed we find that we are over-dependent on others, are too influenced by feelings, and have difficulty functioning where logic is required.

The balance between feeling and logic is important because it allows us to develop a workable relationship between the value we put on ourselves and the need to consider others. Using our logical capabilities we can judge situations without being unnecessarily governed by the needs of others, we can make decisions based on our own conclusions without being too worried about what others think, and we will be able to act quickly and decisively rather than getting lost in a world of 'ifs', 'buts', and 'maybes'. Being aware of, and being able to tap into our feeling function allows us to consider the needs of others, keep limits to logic and be comfortable within the psychological space of other people.

Finding the balance between the individual and the collective is important so that we meet our belonging needs and at the same time our sense of identity remains intact. Self-awareness enables us to be at ease with who we are, to take pride in our individuality and to allow ourselves to be tested against the general reality of the outside world. Knowing who I am, and being happy with that, allows me to put that image of myself up against the world and not be scared that I will not survive. An inflated sense of who I am, what I can do or what I would like to do, means that I have an unreal self-view which will not allow me to become part of the collective in a way that will satisfy me. In the opposite of inflation where people underrate their capabilities and are too governed by the demands of the collective, their individual identity becomes fused with the collective and their individuality becomes so closely allied with the outer world that they have no sense of separateness or autonomy.

In finding the overall balance in our lives it is important to be able to find the balance between our inner real self and our outer false self. The false self or persona is, as we have seen, our agreement with the conventions of society that we will observe certain generalities of behaviour, attitudes and values in order to be able to play an effective role in our world. The inner self is that part of us which is ours and which we prefer to keep from public view. Acknowledging, accepting and integrating this inner part of ourselves into our everyday world, in a way that is satisfying to us, but not damaging to those around us, is an essential part of this balancing act.

Another balance that is required is the balance between work and play. The over-emphasis on work leads to a negation of the feeling side of the personality, it promotes an excessive emphasis on masculine striving, and it provides us with a vehicle for avoiding important issues in our lives. Play on the other hand allows us to re-create, to generate creative energy, and to develop the right side of the brain. Too much play has the effect of taking away our sense of achievement and our sense of providing, and it gives us an unrealistic approach to the world. The balance between work and play allows us to be productive and to enjoy life, to benefit from our achievements and to relax, to contribute to the well-being of the greater world while at the same time satisfying our own selfish needs.

In seeking to find the overall balance in life the need to balance attachment and separation is integral. The basic need of the person for attachment to parents, family, community and place finds expression in the closeness, connection and love which we experience with family, friends and community. It is the fulfilment of this need for attachment which provides the ego strength and emotional independence to separate from parents, family and community in a way that facilitates personal growth and development. Where separation is forced on us before we are ready to cope with it, where separation is for too long a period, or where separation is too stark, the feeling is one of abandonment, isolation and rejection.

This damaging separation has the effect of preventing healthy attachment and inhibiting normal separation, and has negative effects on the ability to establish and maintain relationships.

The ability to be alone with oneself, the ability to be able to live with oneself, and the ability to value solitude, are important requirements in the process of forming relationships and establishing healthy attachments outside of the primary attachments of the family. Having a balance between being able to inhabit one's own space, to have pride in that space, and to defend it, on the one hand, and on the other, needing safe boundaries around that space allows us to feel safe in our own space and yet not to be threatened by sharing that space with others. Being able to live with oneself is a necessary requirement for being able to live in a relationship.

The overriding issue in all of this is the ability to be happy in our own world, to be able to inhabit the world of others, and yet not to feel threatened by the presence of others in our world. The continual merging of emotional contents, the continual connection of people and the continual psychological overlap is part of a healthy orientation to the world about us. But we can only survive in this world if we are happy with who we are, if we know who we are and if we are prepared to put the 'I' we know out into the emotional marketplace of our world. The ego strength to accept others in our world, to engage with them and to expose our inner self to the reality testing of society, comes from within us, and it is by tapping into who we are, what we have to offer and what we hope to become, that we develop this ego strength.

It is about putting the 'I' into 'Us' and not losing it.